only

the

best

KT-456-561

translated by kate whiteman   photographed by martin brigdale   quadrille

only
the
best

the art of cooking with a master chef

michel
roux

Creative Director: Mary Evans
Publishing Director: Anne Furniss
Project Editor: Janet Illsley
Design: Paul Welti
Translator and Editor: Kate Whiteman
Photographer: Martin Brigdale
Stylist: Helen Trent
Production: Nancy Roberts
Design Assistant: Samantha Rolfe
Editorial Assistant: Katie Ginn

First published in 2002 by
Quadrille Publishing Limited
Alhambra House
27-31 Charing Cross Road
London WC2H OLS

Text © Michel Roux 2002
Photography © Martin Brigdale 2002
Design and layout © Quadrille
Publishing Ltd 2002

The rights of Michel Roux as the
author have been asserted.
All rights reserved. No part of this
book may be reproduced, stored in a
retrieval system or transmitted in any
form or by any means, electronic,
electrostatic, magnetic tape,
mechanical, photocopying, recording
or otherwise, without prior permission
in writing from the publisher.

Cataloguing-in-Publication Data: a
catalogue record for this book is
available from the British Library.

ISBN 1 903845 75 0
Printed and bound in Singapore

dedication

I dedicate this book to the artisans whose produce enables
me to cook the way I do. Without them I would lose my
passion. To ensure that the cycle of quality continues, they
steadfastly refuse to compromise their principles. They
work without counting the hours, and are as dedicated to
their products as I am to the finished result on the plate.
I thank you all.

HAMMERSMITH AND WEST
LONDON COLLEGE
LEARNING CENTRE

17 MAR 2003

DAW L621957 £25.00
310497
641.5944 MIC
Arts & Leisure

310497

contents

notes

All spoon measures are level unless otherwise suggested:
1 teaspoon = 5ml spoon, 1 tablespoon = 15ml spoon.
All eggs are medium unless otherwise stated, and I recommend you
use organic or free-range eggs. Those in a vulnerable health group,
including anyone who is pregnant, should avoid those recipes that
contain raw or lightly cooked egg.
Ovens and grills should be preheated to the specified temperature.

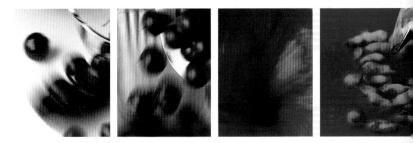

introduction

How intoxicating it feels to participate in the evolution of cooking for the benefit and happiness of all food lovers! Merely moving with the times can be banal and boring, but my five senses come alive when I am involved in the development of new culinary trends. Thanks to an innate desire to create, mine is a progressive style of cooking, based on the natural flavours and qualities of the products I use. I want to give life back to the ingredients I cook, not to neutralise or stifle them with inappropriate techniques or an excessive use of herbs or spices.

Throughout my long career, while creating new menus at The Waterside Inn, writing numerous books and educating hundreds of young cooks and patissiers, professional and non-professional alike, my mantra has always been "modern cuisine, constantly evolving cuisine". Amidst the profusion of gastronomic excesses and tastes of those wannabe culinary stars, some of whom have no real conception of what cooking is about, I can remain serene.

This book reflects my personal aspirations, those of a gourmet who only cooks what he likes to eat. Each chapter guides you through the different cooking methods that have been refined to perfection. The recipes are simple, creative and sophisticated, and accessible to all my readers.

Martin Brigdale's superb step-by-step photography and pictures of the finished dishes will give you the confidence to recreate these recipes; they truly illustrate the originality and inventiveness of the dishes. It gives me enormous pleasure to share with you my understanding of the ingredients and products that are so valuable in the cooking that I do today.

I am passionate about food. Even cooking a simple bowl of rice can evoke a range of emotional responses, as I take in the different aromas arising from Thai jasmine or sticky rice, basmati, arborio, short, long or round grain, and wild rice. Cooking rice to perfection demands skill, and this simple task gives me satisfaction.

I love to experience the refined cuisines of my colleagues, particularly Paul Bocuse, Michel Guérard and Pierre Gagnaire, with their different styles … classical, modern, or eclectic. In their different ways, they all produce something sublime; I adore this, and the emotion it evokes. Cooks are *artistes*; like painters, musicians, sculptors and singers, they all have their own unique style, one is not better than another; they are simply different.

regional produce

I like to find inspiration in local produce, but sadly, it is fast disappearing. Most of our small farmers no longer have local abattoirs where they can send their animals, while producers of vegetables, fruit, cheeses, honey and the like, cannot continue their struggle against the food giants (although, of course, many still battle for survival).

The flood of regulations and directives from Brussels seem designed to ensure that everything that could be good and beautiful is brought to its lowest common denominator. Standardisation is almost forced, to the detriment of quality. Fruit and vegetables are picked weeks before they reach maturity, and are flown on a round-the-world trip or driven the length and breadth of Europe in refrigerated lorries. It doesn't take much imagination to picture the end result on the consumer's plate.

I must admit, I find it hard to keep my cool when I see how the authorities treat European consumers, who have known better and would love to maintain or even improve the quality of the foods they eat. I do, however, find reassurance in the tide of public opposition to genetically modified foods, which are a danger to the consumer, the environment and the inhabitants of the countryside.

Personally, I encourage the use of local organic produce in my kitchens at The Waterside Inn; sadly, I can't use them exclusively, because production is on a small scale, but I do use whatever my local producer can provide even if he only supplies on an occasional basis. Let us hope that good sense will prevail, and that all is not lost! We must continue to fight for what we deserve.

treasures of the sea

The seas, oceans, rivers and lakes that make up almost 70% of our planet provide a huge reservoir of food. Seaweed, for example, adds new iodised flavours to my cooking. I first discovered laverbread over 20 years ago in Wales. More recently, I have been buying marsh and rock samphire from Rungis market to use as a garnish for fish terrines, or in a *salade gourmande* – my seasonal

salad hors d'oeuvre prepared with delicate ingredients fresh from the market. Note that strictly speaking, samphire is not seaweed, but a marine vegetable.

There are many varieties of edible seaweed, all different in appearance, colour and texture. Some have the flavour of dried mushrooms, others of sorrel, oysters or smoked tea; some even have a sweet flavour. In my cooking, seaweed is always used judiciously and parsimoniously, in the same way as spices. It is a subtle ingredient, a sort of condiment, which I mainly use in fish dishes, like salmon en papillote with pine needles (page 137), and my seafood crêpes (page 58). It also features in my croustade with "vegetable spaghetti" (page 173).

At present, the seaweeds I use most often are sea lettuce, dulse, laver, wakame, royal and Breton kombu, and sea spaghetti, which are widely available in health food shops. I love their appearance and taste, and the contemporary, healthy quality they impart to my dishes.

I like to prepare and cook fish using simple techniques that bring out the full intrinsic flavour of the prime ingredient. Baking fish in a salt crust (page 134) is an excellent way to seal in the flavours and highlight the natural perfection of the fish. I love to serve this with a contrasting drizzle of chive oil and lemon wedges (illustrated on page 6). The freshest of fish can be served raw, lightly smoked or cured (see pages 34–7). Freshly caught sea bream, for example, is delicious "cooked" in salt: mix 500g coarse salt with 50g caster sugar and $1/2$ teaspoon crushed peppercorns. Fillet the fish, sprinkle with the salt mixture, wrap in cling film and refrigerate for about 2 hours. Rinse under a trickle of water, pat dry, then slice thinly like smoked salmon. Arrange the slices on a plate for everyone to help themselves and add lemon juice and olive oil to taste. Toasted country bread makes the perfect accompaniment to this wonderfully natural "fisherman's dish".

I realise that I am not alone in choosing to eat more produce from the sea, and that, as we consume ever more of it, we risk

"I intend to promote completely unfamiliar and untried varieties of fish, which will cost far less"

depleting certain marine species. I want to alert consumers to this danger, and encourage them to discover new, hitherto unknown varieties. Until now, I have tended to use only traditional fish in my recipes. In future, I intend to promote unfamiliar and untried fish that will cost far less than sole, monkfish or turbot, which are becoming ridiculously expensive owing to an insatiable demand.

lemon: my favourite

How I admire this unique ingredient. Not only is the lemon the epitome of health, bursting with vitamin C, but it is multifaceted, and has so many wonderful and astonishing uses. I adore the bright yellow colour, compact shape and skin (thin-skinned fruit are my preference). The fragrance, acid juice and extraordinary versatility combine to make the lemon "the king of ingredients" in my eyes. Lemons are my loyal indispensable companions in the kitchen; if they did not exist, I should have to create them, since I use them more than any herb, spice or condiment.

Lemons are grown in many Mediterranean countries, but my favourites come from Amalfi on the southern Italian coast. Sold complete with stalks and some of their leaves, they have an exceptional aroma and flavour that justify their high price. Every part is edible, and I urge you not to eschew them.

I grate the peel and use it to perfume madeleines and fresh pasta; I pare the zests to decorate desserts, and dry or freeze them to perfume beef daubes and sauces in winter; I confit them to make aiguillettes of candied peel coated in chocolate. My guests adore the lemon marmalade that I love to make as a change from the orange variety. Lemon pips are rich in pectin and can be used as a setting agent for other jellies and jams, too.

I often put a lemon peel in the switched-off oven after cooking fish to get rid of the smell, or dry slices to add a note of freshness to a pot-pourri. Even my copper cooking pots enjoy the benefits of lemon; mix the juice with a little fine sand, coarse salt, a few egg whites and the leftover lemon skin, then rub over copper to give it a miraculous shine. The only creatures who fear my trusty favourite are ants; a few small pieces of lemon placed along their trail keeps them at bay until I buy a more noxious deterrent!

The acidity of lemon juice accentuates, enlivens and refines my sauces; even those that aren't asleep are galvanised by the minor whiplash it gives them. It enhances and develops the aromas of fruit coulis and sorbets, like my famous lemon "colonel sorbet" with an added dash of vodka, which is often served at The Waterside Inn. A drizzle of lemon juice squeezed over freshly peeled fruits, like bananas, apples, pears, peaches and avocados, as well as sliced mushrooms, peeled artichoke hearts and many other vegetables, will prevent them from oxidising and turning black on the surface. I also put in a piece of lemon when boiling new potatoes to stop them from bursting.

Lemon juice is sometimes substituted for vinegar in my vinaigrettes, especially for summer salads of tender leaves or thinly sliced mushrooms, and it is used in my marinades for fish to be served raw. A good way to check the freshness of certain shellfish is to squeeze lemon juice on to the flesh; oysters and scallops in particular will contract if they are spanking fresh.

When making caramel, once it has reached the right degree of cooking, I add the juice of a lemon to liquefy it. I store this caramel extract in a bottle to use as a delicious addition to certain desserts, like crème caramel and rice pudding, or instead of sugar to sweeten and flavour crème Chantilly.

On long winter evenings, I love to sip a piping hot grog made with lemon juice, honey and a little rum, topped up with boiling water. By contrast, during my military service in North Africa, I used to make a refreshing hot weather drink by adding a few drops of lemon juice reinforced with a pinch of salt to a glass of lemonade.

I salt lemons to use in North African chicken and fish dishes by making incisions in the fruit and rubbing in salt crystals. My *pieds-noirs* friends cut salted lemons into quarters and serve them with other canapés as *kemia*, the equivalent of Spanish tapas.

"fragrance, acid juice and extraordinary versatility combine to make the lemon the king of ingredients in my eyes"

And that's not all. Lemon juice has soothing qualities. I remember my mother rubbing it into her elbows to soften the skin. Even now, when I finish preparing and cooking a dish, I never fail to rub my hands with the remains of a lemon, then sniff it to enjoy its scent. I am not the only one who appreciates the lemon. Every year, during February in the village of Menton, close to the Italian border in the South of France, the "festival of the lemon" is held and the virtues of this prized citrus fruit are celebrated with great gusto.

liquid gold

Year by year, olive oil plays an increasingly important role in my cooking. The moment I arrive in the South of France, I am inspired by the Mediterranean climate to snatch the bottle of liquid gold from the cupboard, pour a drizzle on to a plate, and dunk a piece of fresh crusty bread. Heaven! Throughout my stay, I completely abandon the *echiré* butter that I use as often as olive oil in a harsher climate.

Olive oil is produced in almost all Mediterranean countries, where it occupies a place of honour and every village boasts that theirs is the best. I enjoy wandering through the local fairs when

olive oils are the main attraction, tasting and comparing. I love them all, although each one is different. Their colours range from greenish-yellow to olive green; each has its unique savour and aroma, density or lightness.

I use the lightest oils for cooking dishes like pan-fried monkfish with red pepper confit (page 142), and reserve the punchier, fruity varieties for marinades for fish that will be served raw. I use it abundantly in my *sauce vierge* and *rouille* for my bouillabaisse; substitute it for cream in a potato purée; confit tomatoes, peppers and garlic in it (see pages 79–80); drizzle it over delicious tiny red mullet or sea bream in a fine salt crust (page 134), and add a slug to fresh pasta with a few basil leaves. And so on ...

Olive oil adds vitality to my cooking, making it more digestible and modern. I never fail to buy a couple of flagons when I find a new producer in a far-flung place; after all, olive trees are not exclusive to the Mediterranean, but grow in other continents. California, Australia and South Africa all produce fine olive oils. One of my favourites, Morgenster, is produced by Giulio Bertrand near Capetown.

I enjoy sharing, discovering, discussing and even arguing about its merits with my colleagues. Like *grands crus* clarets, the price escalates according to whether it is virgin, first pressing, extra virgin, or even classified as AOC (*appellation contrôlée*). The label of these fine oils is often festooned with gold medals that have been won in fiercely contested competitions.

And finally, it has remedial qualities. When visiting a wine-producing region, I swallow a couple of spoonfuls of neat olive oil before embarking on a lengthy wine-tasting session. It lines and soothes my stomach, preventing the heartburn and acidity which are always a possible consequence of these protracted tastings, which can sometimes extend over two or three days ...

As you may have gathered, I am passionate about olive oil – quite an admission for the son of a mother from Normandy, where butter is extolled as king.

culinary equipment

I insist that all my kitchen equipment and utensils are efficient and durable – qualities that are reflected in their price. I only buy the very best ingredients, so my cooking and pâtisserie equipment must be of equally high quality to ensure that my dishes are cooked to perfection. Rather than list a hundred items to equip your kitchen, I prefer to tell you about a few of my favourites. You will find a list of suppliers on page 189.

I am still using many of the knives that I have had since my apprenticeship; some of the Sabatier knives are still in good condition and their blades, which I sharpen regularly, never let me down. For the past ten years, I have favoured Japanese Global knives, which give incomparable high-precision results. There are over fifty different types, each designed for a specific use, but many can be put to multiple use. I recommend that you choose five or ten of the following knives to provide a collection to last a lifetime: 25cm Yanagi sashimi; vegetable; carving; serrated; ham; salmon; filleting; boning; paring; utility. You will also need a sharpener to keep them razor-sharp; I recommend the Global ceramic whetstone for domestic use.

The old cast-iron frying pans our grandmothers used are hard to find nowadays, and sadly not such good quality, so I have made the decision to use non-stick pans. After experimenting with many brands, I now use Tefal in my kitchens at home and at The Waterside Inn. The surface of these durable pans does not scratch easily, and there is a wide choice of shapes and sizes. My omelettes, crêpes and blinis have never been better.

For making stock, I use enormous tinned copper stockpots, which I have had for thirty years. Unfortunately, they need re-tinning every three to six months, and it is very hard to find anyone to perform this onerous task nowadays – another example of a fast-disappearing craft. Gradually, I am replacing these pots with stainless steel stockpots or deep saucepans, with reinforced bases that ensure even heat distribution.

All my shallow vegetable pans, deep sauté pans for meat and small pans for sauces, are made from materials that can withstand fierce heat and cook evenly. They must be strong enough to stand up to daily use by a brigade of twenty chefs. I have chosen the American All-Clad brand, which can cope with occasional ill-treatment, and lasts for at least ten years in a professional kitchen – the equivalent of a lifetime in a domestic environment!

Some years ago, Paul Bocuse introduced me to the Staub brand from Alsace. I use their cast-iron casseroles and the small gratin dishes in which I cook eggahs and the like. Staub also make a self-simmering pan, which uses an ingenious system of evaporation, condensation and spraying that guarantees perfect cooking results.

For twenty years, I have used a Braun hand blender to aerate my sauces, *nages* and bouillons, to make them light and frothy. I use this quality blender every day for pâtisserie, fish and meat dishes and soups, and couldn't live without it.

My collection of small implements includes a little marvel of an asparagus peeler made by Monopol in Germany, which I discovered on a farm in northern France where the grower sold asparagus directly to the public. As you peel the asparagus, it follows the contours of the stalks, making it impossible to break them ... a remarkable gadget.

A small battery-operated weighing scale is, of course, essential. It costs very little, and weighs very precisely, which is useful for spices, sugar, yeast etc. Cooking thermometers are also important, notably oven, sugar and meat thermometers (essential for checking internal temperature). Since no built-in gauge accurately indicates the true temperature inside an oven, I regard an oven thermometer as indispensable when cooking fragile confections like macaroons, choux puffs and meringues.

I could carry on extolling the merits of many other utensils, gadgets and equipment. While others might browse around antique shops, I love to visit the specialist cookshop, Mora, in Paris. It's like Aladdin's cave, and I spend hours there, filling my suitcases with whisks, cutters, spatulas, and so on ... I recommend a visit.

chicken stock

This is used in many sauces and to enrich jus, but it can be served as a bouillon in its own right, with a few tarragon leaves or some lemon grass added.

Makes 1.5 litres

1 boiling fowl, about 1.5kg, or the equivalent weight of chicken carcasses, wings or thighs, blanched and refreshed
2.5 litres cold water
200g carrots, cut into rounds
white part of 2 leeks, thinly sliced
1 onion, peeled and stuck with 2 cloves
200g button mushrooms, thinly sliced
1 large bouquet garni (to include a celery stick)
1 teaspoon crushed peppercorns

Put the chicken in a saucepan, add the water and bring to the boil over a high heat. Immediately lower the heat and simmer gently for 10 minutes, skimming as necessary. Add all the other ingredients. Cook gently allowing 1¹/₂ hours for a whole bird; 50 minutes for pieces or carcasses; skim regularly.

Strain the stock through a fine chinois into a bowl and cool quickly over ice. Refrigerate for up to 5 days.

fish stock

Makes 2 litres

1.5kg chopped bones and/or trimmings of sole, turbot, brill or whiting
50g butter
75g onions, peeled and thinly sliced
white parts of 2 leeks, thinly sliced
75g button mushrooms, thinly sliced
200ml dry white wine
2.5 litres cold water
1 bouquet garni
2 lemon slices
8 white peppercorns, coarsely crushed and tied in a square of muslin

Rinse the fish bones and trimmings under cold running water to remove any blood, and drain.

Melt the butter in a saucepan, add the vegetables and sweat over a low heat for a few minutes. Add the fish bones and trimmings, simmer gently for a few minutes, then add the wine and reduce by two-thirds.

Pour in the water, bring to the boil, then lower the heat to a very gentle simmer and skim. Add the bouquet garni and lemon slices. Simmer gently for 15 minutes, skimming as necessary. Add the peppercorns and simmer for another 10 minutes. Gently ladle the stock through a fine chinois into a bowl and cool over ice, as quickly as possible.

vegetable stock

The vegetables can be varied according to your taste and the season – ripe tomatoes in summer, woodland mushrooms (especially chanterelles) in autumn, and so on. To make a *nage*, which is a light poaching liquid rather than a classic stock, I add a touch of acidity – in this case vinegar.

Makes about 2 litres

300g carrots, peeled and cut into rounds
white parts of 2 leeks, thinly sliced
100g celery stalks, thinly sliced
50g bulb fennel, very thinly sliced
150g shallots, peeled and thinly sliced
100g onion, peeled and thinly sliced
2 unpeeled garlic cloves
1 bouquet garni
250ml dry white wine
2 litres water
10g white peppercorns, coarsely crushed and tied in a square of muslin
3 tablespoons white wine vinegar (only for a nage)

Put all the ingredients in a saucepan. Bring to the boil over a high heat, then lower the heat and simmer gently for 45 minutes, skimming the surface as necessary. Strain through a fine chinois into a bowl and cool over ice, as quickly as possible.

lemon and mint vinaigrette

This refreshing vinaigrette is the perfect foil for watercress and it features in my poached eggs on watercress salad with red pepper salsa (page 54). It also makes an excellent dressing for grated carrot or a warm salad of cooked cauliflower.

Serves 6

2 lemons
6 mint leaves
6 tablespoons groundnut oil
salt and freshly ground pepper

Wash and dry the lemons, finely grate the zest of one, and squeeze the juice of both of them. Roll up the mint leaves and finely snip them.

Put the lemon zest and juice in a bowl with the oil, season with salt and pepper and whisk to mix. Stir in the mint at the very last moment, just before serving.

sherry vinaigrette

This is a superb dressing for crisp salad leaves, like chicory, frisée and dandelion, or for cooked French beans or potatoes that are served warm.

Serves 6

2 eggs
3 tablespoons sherry vinegar
6 tablespoons groundnut oil
2 very thin rashers of streaky bacon, fried until crisp and finely diced
salt and freshly ground pepper

Add the eggs to a pan of boiling water and hard-boil for no longer than 6 minutes. Cool quickly in cold water, then shell and finely chop the eggs, or rub them through a sieve. Put them in a bowl and season with salt and pepper. Whisk in the vinegar, then the groundnut oil. Finally add the bacon.

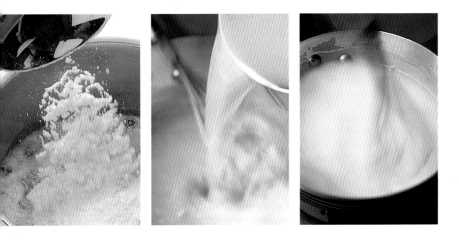

sauce suprême

I sometimes enrich this sauce with egg yolks, particularly if it is to be glazed under the grill. Poached oysters, lightly coated with sauce suprême and glazed under the grill until warm, are divine. I also use the sauce in my seafood crêpes (page 58), illustrated opposite. If you are serving sauce suprême on its own, it will be less rich without the egg yolks.

Makes 1 litre
1 litre velouté sauce (see left)
100ml double cream
2 egg yolks (optional)
2 small pinches of saffron threads (optional)
salt and freshly ground pepper

In a saucepan, gently heat the velouté sauce, stirring occasionally with a whisk. As soon as it comes to the boil, add the cream and egg yolks if using. Allow the sauce to bubble for only 2 minutes if you are using egg yolks, or 5 minutes if not.

Season with salt and pepper to taste, and add the saffron if using, rubbing the threads between your fingertips. Whisk and heat gently until simmering.

velouté sauce

This velvety sauce can be served as it is, but it's also used as the base for sauce suprême (see right) and, in smaller quantities, for other white sauces. The addition of a spoonful or two of velouté will add body to a white wine sauce to accompany fish. It is important to note that if the white roux is hot, the added stock must be cold, and vice-versa, otherwise the sauce will be lumpy.

Makes 1 litre
30g butter
30g plain flour, sifted
1 litre fish stock (page 16), chicken stock (page 16), or vegetable stock (page 17)
salt and freshly ground pepper

First make a white roux. Melt the butter in a heavy-based saucepan. Off the heat, add the flour and stir it in with a whisk. Return to a medium heat and cook for 3 minutes, stirring continuously.

Pour the cold stock on to the roux, stirring all the time, then cook the sauce over a low heat for about 30 minutes, stirring occasionally with a whisk. Season with salt and pepper to taste.

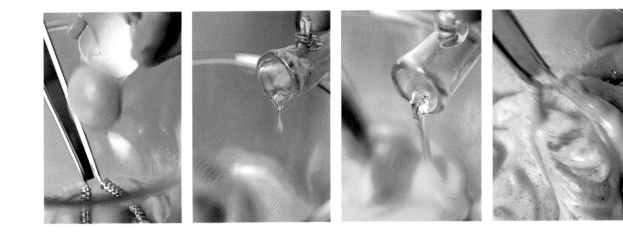

hollandaise sauce

This light, classic sauce is delicate and should be served as soon as it is made, though you can keep it warm for 10–15 minutes. I serve it with grilled lobster with garden herbs (page 119), and my salmon mousse and spinach tartlets (page 70).

Hollandaise is the inspiration for many other sauces. For a noisette sauce to serve with fish, whisk 50g browned butter at room temperature into the hollandaise just before serving.

Serves 6

1 tablespoon white wine vinegar
4 tablespoons cold water
1 teaspoon white peppercorns, crushed
4 egg yolks
250g clarified butter (page 188), cooled to tepid
juice of 1/2 lemon
salt

Put the vinegar, water and pepper in a small pan, set on a low heat and reduce by one-third. Leave until cold.

Add the egg yolks and mix with a whisk. Stand the pan on a heat diffuser over a very low heat and continue to whisk, keeping the whisk in contact with the base of the pan. Still whisking continuously, very gradually increase the heat to no more than 65–70°C, so that the sauce emulsifies extremely slowly; it will take 8–10 minutes to become smooth and creamy.

Off the heat, trickle in the tepid butter, whisking as you go. Season with salt. Stir in the lemon juice at the last moment. Serve at once.

curry mayonnaise

This versatile mayonnaise goes well with crudités, vegetable tempura (page 152), hard-boiled eggs, cold roast chicken, and any cold poached firm-fleshed white fish. You can lighten it by folding in 50–100g fromage frais, or make it creamier by adding 2 tablespoons crème fraîche.

For an original twist on plain mayonnaise, omit the curry powder and add 2 or 3 spoonfuls of reduced tomato coulis. For a mustardy mayonnaise, replace the curry powder with a generous pinch of English mustard powder.

Makes about 300ml

1 tablespoon strong Dijon mustard
2 egg yolks, at room temperature
250ml groundnut oil, at room temperature
1 tablespoon curry powder (mild or hot, to taste)
2 tablespoons lemon juice, or warm wine vinegar
salt and freshly ground pepper

Combine the mustard, salt and pepper in a bowl. Add the egg yolks and immediately mix these ingredients together with a small whisk.

Whisk in the oil, drop by drop to begin with, then in a thin stream, until it is all incorporated.

Dissolve the curry powder in the lemon juice or vinegar and stir it into the mayonnaise. Taste and add more salt and pepper if necessary. Whisk for another 30 seconds to make a thick, glossy mayonnaise.

Serve the mayonnaise immediately, or cover the bowl with cling film and refrigerate for up to 3 hours.

red pepper salsa

I like to serve this salsa with my ham mousse (page 69), but it is equally delicious eaten alone, spread on toast. I prefer to char the peppers on a barbecue (to which I add some vine shoots). If this isn't convenient, blister the skins in a hot oven or under a very hot grill, though the flavour won't be quite as good. If the peppers are not as sweet as they should be, add some chopped confit tomatoes (page 79).

Serves 8

4 red peppers
2 small yellow peppers (optional)
125ml olive oil
2 shallots, peeled and finely chopped
leaves from 2 small thyme sprigs, chopped
10–12 basil leaves, snipped
juice of 2 lemons
salt and freshly ground pepper

Using your fingertips, oil the peppers very lightly. Grill them (preferably on the barbecue) until the skins are blistered and blackened.

Plunge the peppers into a bowl of water filled with ice cubes, then take out and peel off the skin.

Halve the peppers, remove the core and scrape out the white membranes and seeds. Cut the peppers into long thin strips. If you are using yellow peppers, cut them into julienne and set aside to add a final touch of colour to the salsa.

Dice the red peppers as finely as possible and place in a bowl. The texture should be almost pulpy – halfway between tiny dice and a coulis.

Add the shallots, thyme and basil to the red peppers, season with salt and pepper, and stir in the olive oil and lemon juice. Mix carefully, adding the yellow pepper julienne if using.

Serve the salsa immediately, or cover with cling film and keep in the fridge for up to 48 hours.

pear and lime salsa

This makes a delicious accompaniment to my wild boar and morel pâté en croûte (page 73) and all meat-based terrines. It is also good served cold with my terrine of baby vegetables (page 77). The salsa keeps well in the fridge for a week.

Serves 8

Poaching liquid:
500ml water
200g caster sugar
juice of ¹/₂ lemon

Salsa:
2 very ripe pears
30g shallots, peeled and finely chopped
15g cornichons, cut into thin strips
grated zest of ¹/₂ lime
juice of ¹/₂ lime
50ml olive oil
4 very ripe raspberries
salt and freshly ground pepper

Combine the water, sugar and lemon juice in a saucepan. Peel the pears, halve lengthways and remove the cores. Add them to the poaching liquid and bring to the boil. Immediately lower the heat and poach the pears gently until lightly cooked; this will take about 10 minutes, depending how ripe they are. Leave to cool completely in the syrup.

Drain the pears, cut into small dice and place in a bowl. Add the other ingredients, lightly crushing the raspberries with a fork. Season with pepper to taste and add just a pinch of salt.

herb salsa

This salsa goes particularly well with my wild mushroom cappelletti (page 88). You can also serve it with steamed cauliflower or French beans as an hors d'oeuvre, or with grilled tuna.

Serves 6

1 potato, about 60g
60g fines herbes (tarragon, chervil and flat-leaf parsley), snipped
40ml sherry vinegar
120ml olive oil
juice of 1 lemon
30g spring onions, finely chopped
1 tablespoon coarse grain mustard (eg Meaux)
salt and freshly ground pepper

Boil the potato in its skin, then peel and press through the coarse blade of a vegetable mouli or potato ricer.

Combine all the ingredients in a bowl, seasoning with salt and pepper to taste.

green olive and lemon salsa

This is an excellent accompaniment to my tartares of salmon and scallops in chicory leaves (page 40), most cold poached fish and vegetable crudités.

Serves 6

1 potato, about 80g
1 lemon
juice of 2 lemons
12 green olives, pitted and finely diced
1 tablespoon snipped flat-leaf parsley
pinch of saffron threads, infused in 1 tablespoon warm water
100ml olive oil
30g spring onions, finely chopped
salt and freshly ground pepper

Boil the potato in its skin, then peel it and press through the coarse blade of a vegetable mouli or potato ricer. Peel the lemon, cutting off all pith and membrane, then cut it into segments.

Combine all the ingredients in a bowl, seasoning with salt and pepper to taste.

sweet and sour sauce

I like to serve this unusual sauce with langoustine and squid tempura (page 153) and my sashimi (page 37), but it is good with ham and other cold meat dishes too. Veal stock gives a rich depth of flavour, but you can use chicken stock (page 16) or vegetable stock (page 17) and reduce the sauce for longer to intensify the taste.

Stored in an airtight jar in the fridge, sweet and sour sauce will keep well for 2 weeks.

Makes 180–200ml

200g green peppers
200g red peppers
2 tablespoons groundnut oil
200g onions, peeled and finely diced
100g demerara sugar
100ml red wine vinegar
150ml veal stock (homemade or bought)

Skin the peppers as for red pepper salsa (page 22). Halve, core and deseed them, then dice.

Gently heat the oil in a heavy-based saucepan. Add the onions and sweat for 5 minutes, stirring with a wooden spoon. Add the peppers and sweat, stirring, for another 5 minutes. Add the sugar and cook until the vegetables are lightly caramelised, stirring all the time.

Pour in the vinegar and deglaze the pan. When the liquid comes to the boil, reduce it by two-thirds over a medium heat. Add the veal stock and cook until the sauce is reduced and lightly coats the back of a spoon. Serve the sauce tepid or cold.

pesto

Flavoured with basil, pesto is highly aromatic and widely used in Mediterranean cooking to enhance soups, steamed fish and pasta. It keeps well for several days in an airtight container in the fridge. Leave it at room temperature for 30 minutes before serving for optimum flavour.

For a denser, richer pesto, add 30g toasted pine nuts and pulverise them with the basil. This version is delicious stirred into a risotto.

Serves 6
2 garlic cloves, peeled
20 basil leaves
100g parmesan, freshly grated
150ml olive oil
salt and freshly ground pepper

Remove the green germ from the middle of each garlic clove. Put the garlic in a mortar, add a pinch of salt and pound to a paste. Add the basil leaves and pound until very smooth.

Add the parmesan, then trickle in the olive oil, stirring continuously. Season with salt and pepper.

cep coulis

This is excellent with poached or pan-fried poultry or used as a dressing for pasta. Or you can pan-fry ceps with a touch of garlic and parsley until crunchy, and serve them on a little cep coulis as a starter. The contrast of flavours and textures is superb.

Serves 6
75g butter
30g shallot, peeled and chopped
300g fresh ceps, cleaned (or frozen ceps, thawed), finely sliced
300ml chicken stock (page 16)
1 small garlic clove, peeled and crushed
20g flat-leaf parsley, snipped
salt and freshly ground pepper

Melt 50g butter in a saucepan. Add the shallot, then the ceps and sweat over a low heat for 5 minutes. Add the stock, garlic and parsley and cook over a medium heat for 10 minutes.

Tip into a blender and blend for 5 minutes until very smooth, then strain through a chinois.

Just before serving, reheat the coulis. Dice the remaining 25g butter and whisk into the coulis at the last minute; season with salt and pepper, and serve.

cucumber coulis

This refreshing coulis goes very well with cold poached fish, smoked salmon, cold omelettes and pasta salads. It will keep for up to 48 hours in the fridge, but the water in the cucumber will cause it to separate, so stir with a small whisk for a few moments just before serving.

Serves 6

1 medium cucumber
1 small red chilli
4–5 parsley sprigs
6 sage leaves
50ml olive oil
squeeze of lemon juice, to taste
salt and freshly ground pepper

Peel the cucumber, cut it in half lengthways and remove the seeds. Cut the cucumber into chunks and put in a blender.

Halve the chilli lengthways. Scrape out the white membrane and seeds with a small knife, then chop as finely as possible. Add the chilli to the blender. (Remember to wash your hands afterwards.)

Whizz the cucumber chunks and chilli for 1 minute until fairly smooth.

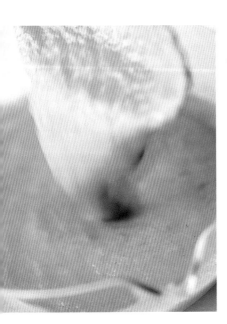

Roughly chop the parsley and sage leaves. Tip them into the blender and process for another minute.

Pour the olive oil into the blender and add a generous squeeze of lemon juice. Blend for about 2 minutes, until smooth and almost creamy. Pour into a bowl. Taste and adjust the seasoning, adding more lemon juice if needed. Cover and refrigerate the coulis until ready to serve.

leek coulis with saffron and dill

This is one of my favourite coulis. It marries well with firm-fleshed fish like brill, monkfish and turbot, or seafood such as langoustine tails and scallops. As with all savoury coulis, you can use vegetable stock rather than chicken stock to satisfy vegetarians.

Serves 6

400g young leeks, greenest parts removed
50g butter
300ml chicken stock (page 16) or vegetable stock (page 17)
2 small pinches of saffron strands
300ml double cream
1 tablespoon chopped dill
salt and freshly ground pepper

Halve the leeks lengthways, wash thoroughly in cold water and slice them finely. Blanch in boiling water for 2 minutes, then refresh in cold water and drain well, pressing the leeks to extract all moisture.

Melt the butter in a saucepan, add the leeks and sweat them gently for 10 minutes. Add the stock, then the saffron, and cook over a medium heat for barely 10 minutes. Add the cream and bubble for 5 minutes.

Tip into a blender and whizz for 2 minutes. Strain through a chinois and season with salt and pepper.

Keep the coulis warm if it is to be served soon; otherwise reheat it gently just before serving. Stir in the dill at the very last moment.

saffron mango coulis

Serves 6

250g mango flesh, cut into chunks
juice of 1 lemon
250ml sugar syrup (page 188)
pinch of saffron threads (about 3g)

Purée the mango in a blender with the lemon juice and half of the sugar syrup, then pass through a fine chinois.

Heat the remaining sugar syrup in a small saucepan, add the saffron threads and bring to the boil. Take off the heat and leave to cool. When cold, whisk the syrup into the mango coulis. Cover and refrigerate until needed.

gingered pear coulis

Serves 6

3 very ripe pears, each 200g
150ml water
150g caster sugar
juice of 1/2 lemon
10g fresh ginger, peeled and very thinly sliced

Peel and core the pears, and cut into pieces. Place in a saucepan with the water, sugar and lemon juice, and bring to the boil. Lower the heat and poach the pears for 5–10 minutes, depending on their ripeness. Add the ginger and cook for 1–2 minutes, then leave to cool.

Blitz the cold pear mixture in a blender for 1 minute, then pass through a fine chinois into a bowl; refrigerate until ready to use. If the coulis seems too thick, dilute it with a few spoons of cold water or, better still, port.

redcurrant and passion fruit coulis

Icing sugar gives this coulis a brilliance, which you cannot achieve with caster sugar. I love to include passion fruit seeds, which float attractively in the clear liquid coulis.

Serves 4–6

200g redcurrants
150–200g icing sugar, sifted
1 passion fruit, halved

Run the prongs of a fork down the central stem to strip the redcurrants from their stalks.

Put the redcurrants into a blender or food processor and whizz for 2 minutes.

Tip the redcurrant purée into a muslin-lined sieve over a bowl to strain the juice.

When most of the redcurrant juice has passed through, gather two corners of the muslin in each hand and twist in opposite directions to extract the remaining juice.

Gradually whisk in the icing sugar – keep tasting the coulis as you add it – the amount you need will depend on the ripeness of the redcurrants.

Pour the redcurrant coulis on to the serving plate. Scoop out the passion fruit seeds and pulp and scatter them over the coulis.

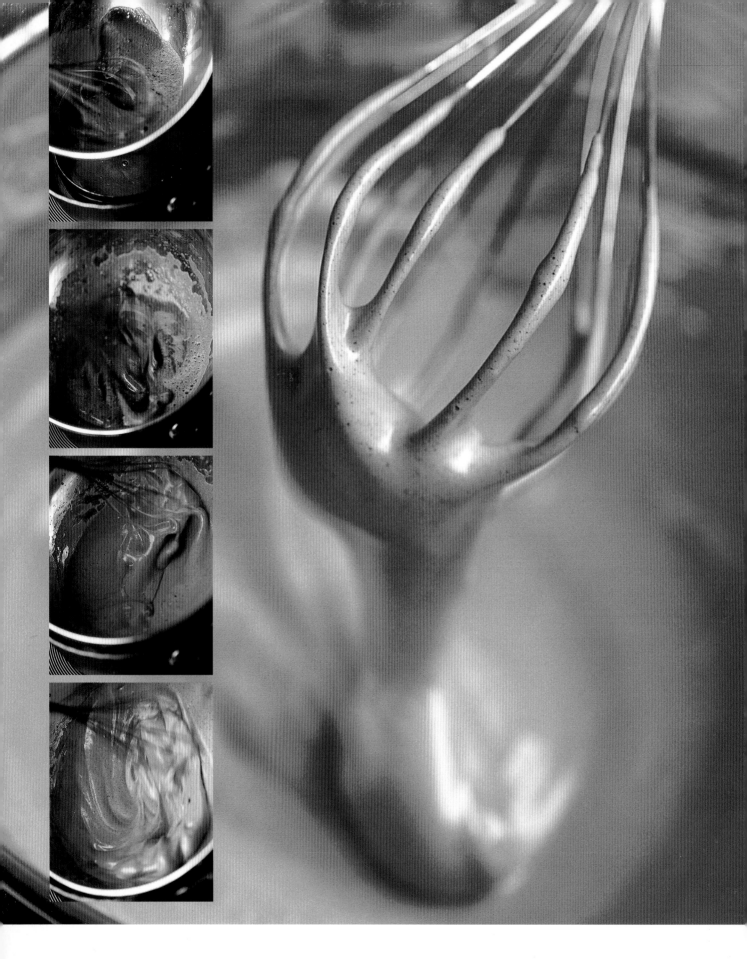

coffee sabayon
with cinnamon

This sabayon is really a dessert in itself, but it also makes a tempting sauce to serve with fresh orange segments or poached pears (drained of their syrup). I like to serve it simply with lacy orange tuiles – they provide a perfect contrast to the creaminess and fragrance of the sabayon. The hint of cinnamon adds a spicy note and enhances the aroma of the coffee.

Serves 4

1 tablespoon instant coffee
60ml cold water
4 egg yolks
50g caster sugar
1/2 teaspoon ground cinnamon

To serve (optional):

orange tuiles (page 185)

For your bain-marie, half-fill a saucepan that is large enough to hold a round-bottomed copper bowl or pan (or a heatproof glass bowl) with warm water. Place the saucepan over a low heat.

Put the coffee and cold water in the bowl and whisk with a balloon whisk to dissolve. Lightly whisk in the egg yolks, sugar and cinnamon.

Set the bowl in the bain-marie and continue to whisk the mixture without stopping for 10–12 minutes. It will thicken and increase dramatically in volume as air is incorporated. The sabayon is ready when it is light, fluffy and shiny, and thick enough to leave a dense ribbon when the whisk is lifted. The water in the bain-marie must not exceed 90°C, or the sabayon will start to coagulate; the temperature of the sabayon itself must not go above 65°C. If necessary, turn off or reduce the heat as you whisk.

Serve the sabayon in glasses as soon as it is ready, with orange tuiles if you like.

chocolate sauce

The sauce is delicious served with poached pears, vanilla or coffee ice cream, meringues, profiteroles or a banana tart. A dash of Grand Marnier will enhance it and add a sweet spiritous touch.

Serves 6

200ml milk
2 tablespoons double cream
40g caster sugar
1/4–1/2 teaspoon cardamom seeds, crushed
200g bitter chocolate (minimum 70% cocoa solids), or dark couverture, cut into pieces
30g softened butter, at room temperature

Put the milk, cream and sugar in a saucepan and bring to the boil, stirring continuously. As soon as the milk begins to boil, put in the cardamom seeds, turn off the heat, cover the pan, and leave to infuse for 5 minutes.

Melt the chocolate in a bowl over a pan of hot water, or in the microwave, stirring until smooth. Strain the milk mixture through a fine chinois on to the chocolate, stirring with a whisk.

Whisk in the butter, a small piece at a time, to make the sauce smooth and glossy. It is now ready to serve.

chocolate sauce
scented with tobacco

I learned of the affinity between chocolate and tobacco from my friend Michel Rostang, who combines them in one of the petits fours he serves in his restaurant in Paris. If the idea of eating tobacco alarms you, rest assured that tobacco leaves are harmless until lit.

Simply infuse the milk mixture with 5g top-quality Havana or San Dominican cigar leaves rather than cardamom seeds. If you find the tobacco flavour a little too pungent, a dash of Grand Marnier will modify it.

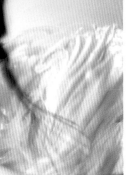
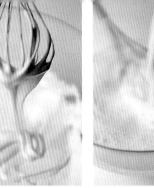
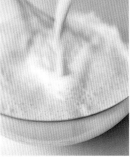

pistachio crème anglaise

This unusual custard – delicately flavoured and coloured with pistachios – is superb with my poached white peaches (page 107) illustrated opposite, and poached pears in sauternes (page 108). Naturally, you can use other flavourings in place of the pistachios.

For a classic crème anglaise, infuse the milk with a split vanilla pod. Or try infusing it with a bunch of fresh mint; 20g peeled and finely sliced fresh peeled root ginger; or 4 or 5 star anise.

Alternatively, flavour the milk with 60g melted bitter chocolate, or 2 tablespoons instant coffee. And of course, you can churn and freeze crème anglaise to make a superb ice cream.

Makes about 750ml

200g shelled pistachios, skinned, or 40g
pistachio paste
6 egg yolks
125g caster sugar
500ml milk

If using fresh pistachios, soak them in cold water for 24 hours. The following day, drain the pistachios and crush to a paste using a pestle and mortar.

Put the egg yolks in a bowl and whisk in about one-third of the sugar.

Continue whisking until the mixture becomes pale and has a ribbon consistency.

Put the milk and remaining sugar in a saucepan, stir and bring to the boil, then pour the boiling milk on to the egg and sugar mixture, whisking continuously.

Pour the mixture back into the saucepan and heat gently, stirring continuously with a wooden spoon, until the custard is about 80°C and thick enough to coat the back of the spoon. When you run a fingertip down the back of the spoon, it should leave a trail in the custard. Immediately take off the heat.

Pour one-third of the custard on to the pistachio paste, stirring continuously with a whisk, then stir this mixture back into the custard in the pan.

Pour the custard into a blender and blend for about 3 minutes, until very smooth.

Pass the custard through a fine chinois into a bowl, set the bowl over crushed ice and leave to cool, stirring occasionally with a wooden spoon to prevent a skin forming. When cold, cover the surface with cling film and refrigerate (for up to 48 hours) until ready to use.

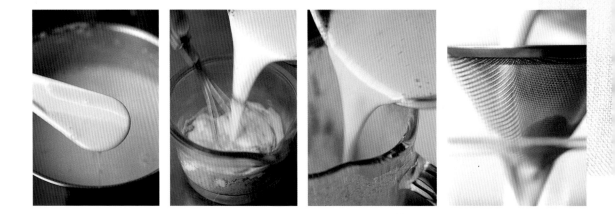

raw and cured food

I am always fascinated by the extreme freshness of the fish that Japanese chefs use to prepare sashimi. I uphold their maxim that the best method of cooking fish that is so fresh is not to cook it at all. Unfortunately, all too frequently, the fish sold in supermarkets has been frozen; this alters the flavour and texture, a fact which my palate never fails to detect when I eat a plate of sashimi. My fishmonger (see page 192), who specialises in fish for sashimi, provides me with the freshly caught fish that are often so difficult to obtain.

carpaccio of shellfish. You need an acid ingredient to do the "cooking"; I most often use lemon juice, but occasionally choose a little fresh tomato juice or a few drops of fresh pineapple juice. I might even use a top quality, delicate vinegar such as raspberry, full of the aromas of red berries, or in winter, a cider vinegar redolent of apples. If the flavour demands, I sometimes add a teaspoon of clear lavender honey or maple syrup, which impart subtle, simply divine flavours.

I regard olive oil as the diva of flavourings. I prefer first pressing extra virgin olive oil, and use it sparingly to avoid drowning the taste of the main ingredient. Use it plain, or flavoured with a few chives (page 188), basil, perhaps even lemon verbena.

Salt, lemon, sugar and pepper reign supreme in this chapter, as they are the essential elements of curing and drying. I also explain two ways of smoking. The first is in my lightly smoked duck breasts (page 44), in which orange zests, star anise and demerara sugar infuse the duck with mellow, sweet and spicy aromas. In the second method, I smoke a sea bass fillet (page 47) using a little sawdust – oak, beech or chestnut, according to taste. I love to smoke certain foods in this way, but only very lightly so that the taste of wood is not discernible. Sadly, commercially smoked foods, like duck and chicken, are often over-smoked in order to disguise their inferior flavour. The same principle applies in wine-making; there is no need to over-oak a fine wine…

For cooking without heat, I use the Tahitian method, applying it to raw fish tartares, like my tartares of salmon and scallops (page 40), scallops marinated in lemon-scented olive olive oil (page 39) and a

Tartares and carpaccios prepared *à la tahitienne* must be served at once to preserve all their flavours. If they are prepared too long in advance, the flavours dissipate. I often serve mini dishes of these fish and shellfish as *amuse-bouches* "compliments of the chef". The delicate taste of the half-cooked seafood sharpens the appetite before a meal.

The technique of curing with salt, with its preservative and antibacterial qualities, dates from the dawn of time. I prefer the dry-salting method, which I apply for only a short time. It draws a natural brine to the surface of the food, which must be rinsed with cold water and patted dry before serving as it is, or cooking.

To finish, I repeat: give your imagination free reign, but don't forget one vital point. Whatever kind of fish, seafood or meat you intend to salt, cure or smoke, it must be as fresh as can be. Not only will it taste much better, but think of the risks you run if it is not absolutely spanking fresh …

michel's sashimi

I think of sashimi as a kind of modern meat fondue, in which everyone dips the pieces of fish into the sauce of their choice; the only difference being that the fish for sashimi is eaten raw, while the meat for a fondue is fried in oil.

As with all sashimi and sushi, the fish and scallops must be of the freshest and finest quality, and it is essential to keep them in the coldest part of the fridge before slicing. For this, you need a knife with a thin, extremely sharp blade or, better still, a special sashimi or sushi knife.

The carrots, daikon and ginger act as palate-cleansers between bites of each variety of fish dipped into the different sauces. I hope my Japanese colleagues will forgive me this fantasy.

Serves 4

100g daikon (white radish)
100g carrots
150g salmon fillet, skinned
150g red tuna or bonito fillet, skinned
150g albacore tuna, skinned
1 sea bream fillet, skinned if preferred
2 mackerel fillets
2 large scallops
2 small onions, preferably red, peeled
1 lime

Condiments:

wasabi
soy sauce
extra virgin olive oil
pickled ginger
sweet and sour sauce (page 24)
Maldon salt flakes
cracked pepper

Chill 4 serving plates in the fridge. Peel the daikon and carrots and cut into very thin strips, using a mandoline if possible. Place in separate bowls of cold water with some ice cubes.

Cut the salmon and tuna into slices, about 5mm thick. Slice the bream, mackerel and the scallops as thinly as possible – the slices should only be about 2mm thick.

Slice the onions into thin rings. Slice the lime, then quarter each slice.

To serve, arrange 3 or 4 slices of each kind of fish and scallop elegantly on each chilled plate. Add little piles of daikon and carrot strips, the lime and a few onion rings. Finally add the different condiments. Serve immediately, or cover with cling film and refrigerate for no more than a few minutes before serving.

gravadlax of halibut

While cruising in Alaska, I developed this idea for curing halibut – in a similar way to the ubiquitous salmon gravadlax. It tastes superb, especially with my pear and lime salsa (page 23), and a warm potato salad peppered with watercress leaves. The halibut will keep for a week in the fridge, provided you slice it only just before serving.

Serves 8

1 very fresh halibut fillet on the skin (preferably the dark skin, as the fillets are thicker), about 1kg
200g fine sea salt
200g caster sugar
30g white peppercorns, finely crushed
60g extra strong Dijon mustard
120g dill, finely chopped, plus 30g for garnish
50ml Cognac
2 lemons, quartered, to garnish

Make sure that there are no small bones left in the halibut fillet. Rinse the fish in cold water and pat dry. Make 4 evenly spaced, small diagonal incisions across the middle two-thirds of the fillet on the skin side; the incisions in the thickest part should be deeper.

Mix the salt with the sugar. Put some of this mixture into each incision, with a little crushed pepper, and press lightly with your thumb. Brush each incision with a little mustard, and press on a little chopped dill.

Turn the halibut fillet over, sprinkle with the rest of the pepper, and press firmly to make it adhere. Brush the whole surface with the remaining mustard, sprinkle with the dill, and moisten with the Cognac.

Scatter the remaining salt and sugar mixture generously over the halibut, putting a greater concentration on the thickest parts of the fillet, and very little on the thinner tail end.

Lay a sheet of cling film (large enough to enclose the halibut in a double thickness) on the work surface. Turn the fillet over on to the cling film, and wrap it up. Place the fish on a tray in the fridge, with a wooden board or baking tray on top to exert a light pressure.

To serve, remove the cling film. Rinse the halibut under cold running water and use your fingertips to check that all the salt and sugar mixture and most of the dill is washed off. Dry the halibut thoroughly on a tea-towel, sprinkle the flesh side with the dill reserved for the garnish, and press with your fingertips to make it adhere.

Using a very sharp, fine-bladed knife, slice the halibut very thinly, as you would smoked salmon, and serve on individual plates, with lemon wedges.

marinated mackerel diamonds

These can be served as a warm hors d'oeuvre; leave them in the marinade for only 30 minutes, then steam them for 3–5 minutes, depending on their thickness. Boiled baby new potatoes make a good accompaniment.

Serves 6

6 mackerel fillets
1/2 lemon
10 juniper berries, lightly crushed
leaves from 1 thyme sprig
1 quantity sweet–sour marinade (page 14)
salt and freshly ground pepper

Pull out any pin bones from the mackerel with tweezers, then cut the fillets into large diamonds and put them in a deep dish. Season lightly.

Cut the lemon half vertically through the middle, then slice it into thin semi-circles. Place these in between the mackerel diamonds, then scatter over the crushed juniper and thyme.

Pour the marinade over the mackerel diamonds. Cover with cling film and leave at room temperature until completely cold, then refrigerate for 2–3 hours.

Serve the mackerel straight from the dish, allowing everyone to season their own fish. Freshly toasted rustic bread is the perfect accompaniment.

PREPARING SCALLOPS

Hold the shell flat-side down with the fingertips of one hand. Using your other hand, slide a rigid knife blade between the two shells.

Carefully run the blade along the inner surface of the flat shell to detach and separate the scallop from the shell.

Lift off the top shell. Slide a spoon or a small palette knife under the scallop in the concave shell, and remove it.

Using your thumb and forefinger, pull away the frilly membrane, and remove the small muscle attached to the scallop. Detach the coral.

The scallop is now ready to use. Rinse it under cold running water. The coral can be used separately or with the scallop, depending on your chosen recipe.

   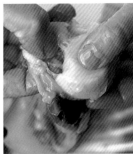 

scallops marinated in lemon-scented olive oil

Crisp textured, finely sliced, raw courgette contrasts beautifully with the melting softness of sliced scallops. For a special occasion, try replacing the salt flakes with grains of caviar ... and enjoy the accolade from your guests.

Serves 4

8 very fresh white scallops, total weight about 480g
120ml olive oil
juice of 3 lemons
20g snipped basil
3 small, long, firm courgettes
3 oranges, preferably blood oranges
Guérande or Maldon salt flakes
salt and freshly ground pepper

Cut the scallops into 3mm thick slices and spread them in a single layer on a tray. Season very lightly with salt and generously with pepper. Mix 75ml of the olive oil with the lemon juice and sprinkle evenly over the scallop slices. Cover with cling film, and refrigerate for 10 minutes.

Turn the scallop slices, one at a time, in the marinade then scatter on the basil. Cover again with cling film and refrigerate for 5 minutes.

Meanwhile, score along the length of the courgettes with a canelle knife, several times to make evenly spaced grooves, then cut into 2–3mm slices. Peel and segment the oranges, discarding all pith.

To serve, arrange 6 orange segments in a rosette in the centre of each plate, and place the courgette discs around them. Sprinkle with a little olive oil and scatter on a few salt flakes, then place a scallop slice on each courgette disc. Serve immediately.

Salmon tartare:

240g skinless middle-cut salmon fillet
20g cornichons, very finely diced
10g dill, finely snipped, plus extra for garnish
4 tender green spring onion leaves, finely snipped
50ml chive oil (page 188)
lemon juice, to taste

To serve:

$^{1}/_{2}$ cucumber
4 red chicory leaves
4 white chicory leaves
4 lemon verbena sprigs (optional)
$^{1}/_{2}$ quantity green olive and lemon salsa (page 24), optional

tartares of salmon and scallops in chicory leaves

I love this unusual presentation. Serving the two tartares in different coloured chicory leaves makes an attractive contrast, though you can of course use all one colour. As with all raw dishes, the ingredients for these tartares must be perfectly fresh. Serve within half an hour of preparation, to preserve the fresh flavours. You can adjust the quantity of lemon juice to suit your taste. I like to drizzle a little green olive and lemon salsa over the two tartares for a touch of piquancy.

Serves 4

Scallop tartare:

4 scallops, in the shell if possible
1 teaspoon dried pink peppercorns
10g chives, finely snipped
20g small capers
30ml orange oil (page 188)
lemon juice, to taste
salt and freshly ground pepper

To make the scallop tartare, open the scallops and remove the white meat (see page 39); you should have about 240g. Cut the scallops into very thin slices, about 3mm thick. Cut these slices into 3mm strips, then into 3mm dice. Place in a bowl.

Lightly crush the pink peppercorns between your fingertips and sprinkle over the scallops. Add the chives, capers, orange oil, and lemon juice to taste. Season lightly with salt and pepper. Stir carefully to mix, cover with cling film and keep in the fridge until ready to serve.

For the salmon tartare, cut the salmon into 3mm dice (in the same way as the scallops). Place in a bowl, add the diced cornichons, snipped dill, onion leaves, chive oil, and lemon juice to taste. Season lightly with salt and pepper. Mix with a spoon, cover with cling film and refrigerate until needed.

Peel, halve and deseed the cucumber. Cut the cucumber flesh into long thin "spaghetti" shreds. Make a little pile of cucumber spaghetti on each serving plate.

Trim the chicory leaves to form canoe shapes. Fill the red leaves with scallop tartare, and the white leaves with salmon tartare. Place one of each colour on each serving plate and scatter a little dill over the salmon tartare. Garnish the plate with lemon verbena if available. Spoon the salsa (if serving) into tiny dishes and place on the plates.

escabèche

Escabèche originated in the Mediterranean and is traditionally prepared with fish from that region, such as sardines and anchovies. When game is in season, I make an innovative version, using partridge breasts or tiny plump quail, adjusting the marinating and cooking times accordingly.

Serves 6

6 very fresh small sardines
6 very fresh anchovies
60ml olive oil
salt and freshly ground pepper

Marinade:

1 lemon
100g carrots, peeled
60g shallots, peeled
50ml olive oil
1 tablespoon white peppercorns, crushed
leaves from a large thyme sprig
2 bay leaves
2 garlic cloves, peeled and crushed
1 tablespoon coriander seeds, crushed
pinch of cayenne pepper
100ml top quality white or red wine vinegar
400ml water

Gently scrape off the scales from the sardines with your thumbnail. Cut off the heads with a knife and slit open the belly, leaving the tail intact. Push out the guts with your thumb and lift out the backbone with your fingers, or a knife. Prepare the anchovies in the same way; there is no need to scale them.

Wipe the sardines and anchovies with a damp cloth, lay them skin-side down on the work surface and open out like a book or butterfly. Season with salt and pepper.

Heat the olive oil in a deep frying pan set over a high heat. Put in the butterflied sardines, skin-side down, and quickly colour them over a high heat for 30 seconds. Lift them out with a slotted spatula on to the serving platter and leave at room temperature.

Repeat with the anchovies, colouring them for 15 seconds. Discard the oil left in the pan.

For the marinade, cut the lemon into 2mm slices, discarding the ends. Cut grooves along the length of the carrots using a canelle knife, then cut into thin rounds. Finely slice the shallots.

Heat the olive oil in the frying pan. Add the shallots and carrots and sweat over a medium heat for a minute or two. Add all the other marinade ingredients, bring to the boil and bubble for 1 minute. Skim the surface if necessary, season very lightly with salt, then pour the boiling marinade over the sardines and anchovies. Leave until cold, then refrigerate for 2–3 hours.

Bring the escabèche to room temperature half an hour before serving. Bring the dish to the table and let everyone help themselves. Put a slice of country bread on the edge of each serving plate.

carpaccio of ceps

Ceps in prime condition are essential for this simple dish, which makes a delicious, light hors d'oeuvre.

Serves 6

12 very fresh, firm-textured ceps, preferably small boletus
juice of 2 lemons
150ml olive oil
30g shallot, peeled and finely chopped
2 lemon thyme sprigs, leaves stripped
150g tomatoes, peeled, deseeded and finely diced
100g very dry chorizo, skinned
2 tablespoons snipped flat-leaf parsley
salt and freshly ground pepper

Using a small knife, trim the cep stalks, and cut off any traces of earth, or impurities. Wipe the ceps gently with a slightly damp cloth, and refrigerate.

In a bowl, mix the lemon juice, olive oil, shallot, thyme leaves and diced tomatoes with a little salt.

When ready to serve, cut the ceps into 2mm slices. Arrange them attractively on serving plates and drizzle with the dressing. Using a parmesan grater, grate the chorizo over the top. Sprinkle with the parsley and a grinding of pepper. Serve chilled.

lightly smoked duck breasts with pak choi

My travels to the Far East have influenced my cooking in recent years. Smoking duck breasts accentuates their fine flavour and the oriental aromatics add a special something. This utterly sublime dish is excellent for lunch or dinner.

You will need a heavy casserole, about 30cm in diameter and at least 15cm deep, with a tight-fitting lid; a 10–20cm flan ring and a 25cm round wire rack. It is essential to protect the base and lid of the casserole with foil, as the sugary smoke could damage them.

Serves 4

4 boned Gressingham or Challandais duck breasts
coarse sea salt
coarsely crushed peppercorns
20g star anise (about 6)
2 dried orange zests, about 20g (see page 113)
500g demerara sugar
600g pak choi or Chinese cabbage
1 red pepper
50ml sugar syrup (page 188)
3 tablespoons untoasted sesame oil
salt and freshly ground pepper

Half an hour before smoking the duck breasts, make criss-cross incisions all over the skin with the tip of a knife. Sprinkle with salt and crushed peppercorns and set aside. Grind the star anise, dried orange zest and demerara sugar together in a spice grinder or food processor to a fine powder.

To prepare the smoker, line the base and underside of the casserole lid with foil. Put in the flan ring, then sprinkle the ground spice mixture over the foil. Place the wire rack on the ring.

Wipe off the excess salt and pepper from the duck breasts and arrange them skin-side up on the rack. Put on the lid and place the casserole over a high heat. As soon as a light smoke seeps out, reduce the heat and cook for 8–10 minutes.

Take off the heat and move the lid slightly so as to barely uncover the casserole. Leave for 10 minutes, then transfer the duck breasts to a plate.

Blanch the pak choi in boiling water for 30 seconds–1 minute, depending on size. Drain thoroughly. Halve, core and deseed the red pepper, then cut into julienne. Heat the sugar syrup in a pan, add the red pepper and simmer for 3 minutes to candy; drain.

Heat the sesame oil in a wok and stir-fry the pak choi for 3–4 minutes, keeping it crunchy. Add the red pepper julienne and turn off the heat.

To serve, cut the duck lengthways into thin slices, using a sharp knife. Arrange the pak choi on one side of each serving plate and fan out the sliced duck breasts alongside. Serve immediately.

smoked chicken wings

Chicken wings can be smoked in the same way as duck breasts (above), allowing an extra 4 minutes smoking. Just before serving, I brush the wings with runny honey, lightly flavoured with lemon juice and a pinch of cayenne, and glaze them under a hot grill for 5 minutes. Finally, I sprinkle them with toasted sesame seeds. They are delicious served on their own as nibbles, or with salad leaves as a starter.

lightly smoked mussels

These delicately smoked mussels are divine tossed with pasta and served drizzled with pesto (see page 88), as illustrated. They can also be added at the last moment to a seafood risotto (page 94). For a light, refreshing starter, toss them in a lemon and mint vinaigrette (page 17) and serve with tomato wedges and frisée (curly endive).

The mussels can be smoked several hours in advance. Cover them with cling film so that they don't dry out, keep in the fridge and steam for a few minutes just before serving.

Serves 4 as a starter

1kg live Bouchot or Shetland mussels
10g star anise (about 3)
10g dried lemon zest, from 1 lemon (see page 113)
250g demerara sugar

Scrub the mussels, wash in several changes of water and drain. Grind the star anise, dried lemon zest and demerara sugar together in a spice grinder or food processor to a fine powder.

Prepare the smoker as for lightly smoked duck breasts (page 44). Put in the mussels and smoke for 6–8 minutes, until they have all opened, then turn off the heat and move the lid very slightly so as to barely uncover the casserole. After about 10 minutes, shell almost all of the mussels, keeping a few in the half-shell for garnish. Discard any unopened mussels.

lightly smoked scallops

Follow the method for lightly smoked mussels (above), allowing 4–6 minutes smoking, depending on the size of the scallops. The smoked scallops can be steamed for 3–4 minutes, or pan-fried in clarified butter (page 188) for 2–3 minutes, again depending on size. To serve, spread a spoonful of my herb salsa (page 24) on a plate, top with the scallops, and surround with mâche (lamb's lettuce) or rocket leaves.

smoked sea bass with chive nage

Light smoking brings out the flavour of this fish, and subtly permeates it with the aroma of the wood. It makes a delicious light lunch or dinner.

You will need about 1kg barbecue briquettes, and 2 handfuls of oak, beech or chestnut sawdust.

Serves 4

1 very fresh unskinned fillet of sea bass, about 600g
400g fine sugar snaps, topped and tailed
30g chives, snipped
75g butter, finely diced
5 lemon wedges
salt and freshly ground pepper

Check that there are no bones left in the fish; rinse and pat dry. Make 6 evenly spaced small diagonal incisions across the middle two-thirds of the fillet on the skin side.

Put the briquettes in a metal shovel under a direct heat source, or into a lit barbecue. When glowing, put in the smoker box and sprinkle with sawdust. Lay the fish, skin-side down, on the grill of the smoker, close the box lid and leave for 10–20 minutes, according to the degree of smoking desired. Lift the fish on to a wire rack and let stand for 15 minutes. If not using at once, wrap in cling film and refrigerate for up to 24 hours.

To cook the fish, cut it into 4 portions. Half-fill a steamer pan with water and salt lightly. Bring to the boil, lower the heat to a simmer and position the top part of the steamer. Put in the sea bass pieces, skin-side down, season, cover and steam for 3–4 minutes. Add the sugar snaps and cook for another 2–3 minutes. To check if the fish is cooked, insert a fine knife tip into the thickest part for 10 seconds; it should penetrate easily, and feel hot when you take it out.

For the sauce, put 75ml of the cooking water in a small pan and reduce by one-third. Add the chives and whisk in the butter, a piece at a time. Squeeze in the juice from 1 lemon wedge; season to taste.

Serve the fish with the chive sauce poured over, and accompanied by the sugar snaps and lemon wedges.

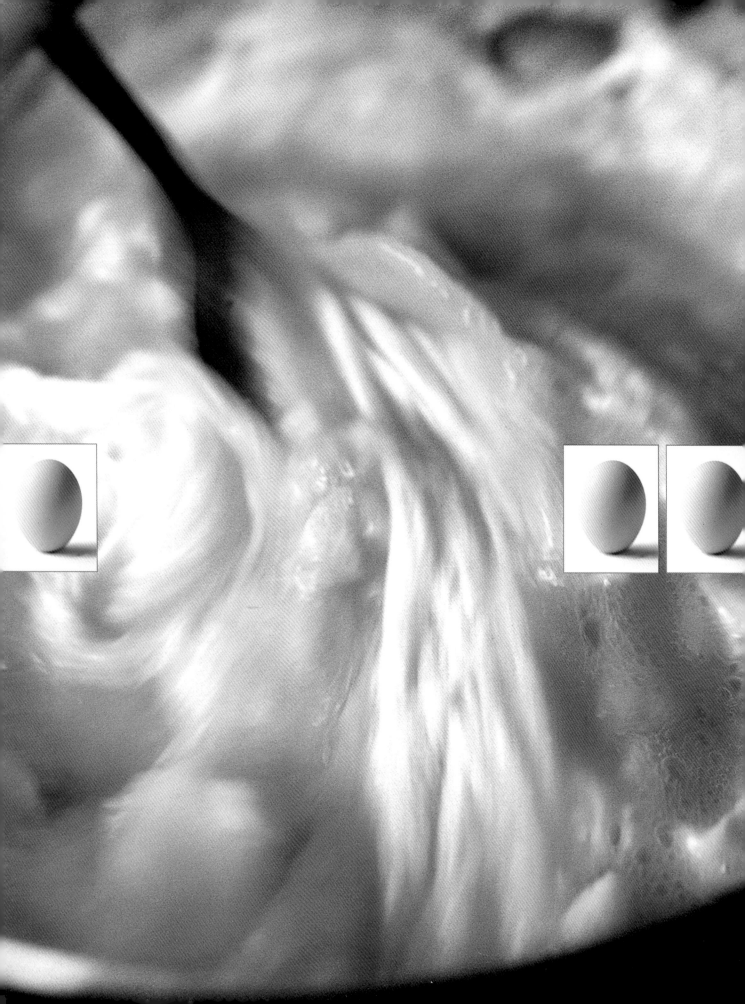

eggs, crêpes and soufflés

At the age of barely three, each time I heard our solitary hen Julie cackle that she was about to lay, I would rush to collect the still-warm egg and take it to my mother, cradling it gently in both hands. I was always surprised and fascinated by the warmth of a new-laid egg. I had no idea then that the egg and I would develop such a long and fruitful partnership throughout my life. An egg is a rich, concentrated source of nutrients – a meal in itself – and I love and respect it in all its forms. In fact I eat about twenty eggs a week in one guise or another.

It is always important to use very fresh eggs. To check the freshness, I pour a litre of water into a bowl, add 100g salt and put in two or three eggs. If they roll around on the bottom, they are ultra-fresh; if they float slightly, they are a few days old, but still useable, but if they float on the surface, I throw them away.

Sugar and salt are the enemies of raw egg yolks and will burn them on contact unless you beat them immediately with a whisk or fork. As for the whites, the white of a new-laid egg will not rise properly when beaten, but one that has been refrigerated for several days will puff up into a perfect snow. Frozen whites can be beaten even stiffer, so I recommend that you freeze any leftover egg whites to use for meringues, macaroons, mousses and of course, soufflés.

During my military service in Algeria, I learnt how to master delicious flat omelettes called eggah. Now I compose all sorts of seasonal variations – a veritable waltz of tortillas, frittatas and eggah. According to what is fresh in the market, I make them with asparagus tips, fresh anchovy fillets or confit aubergines, to serve cut into wedges with a little tomato coulis, as *mezze*; simplicity itself on a plate.

When making soufflés, it is important to use the correct amount of egg white; too little and it won't rise properly, resulting in a heavy texture; too much, and it will taste horribly bland. To be sure of achieving the desired flavour and lightness, I find it more precise to weigh the egg whites rather than count them, because eggs vary in weight so much. I base my soufflés on an average 60g egg (comprising 20g yolk, 35g white and 5g shell). If a soufflé calls for 4 egg whites, for example, you need 140g in total. My advice is to keep a cool head and treat a soufflé like any other dish. They are easy and docile; just follow the technique and method that I use. My visitor's book is full of eulogies extolling my soufflés ... one lady guest remarked that her soufflé was better than an orgasm!

Making crêpes couldn't be easier. All you need is a frying pan, preferably non-stick. Cook the crêpes, pile them on a plate and let them perfume your kitchen. Fill savoury herb crêpes (page 58) with little treasures, like seafood, tomatoes or confit peppers and serve them warm – delicious! Or cover sweet crêpes with grated chocolate or jam, roll up and watch children devour them. To make edible baskets for serving ice cream and sorbet, brush one side of a thin sweet crêpe with melted couverture chocolate, drape it in a bowl, coated-side inwards, and leave until hardened to form a coupe. Fill with ice cream, sorbet or orange segments topped with candied peel.

creamy scrambled eggs with baby vegetables à la grecque

This combination may seem surprising, but it makes an attractive spring or summer dish, and the flavour is sublime. It should be served cold, not chilled. Any spare dressing can be kept in a sealed jar in the fridge for at least a week.

Serves 4

A la grecque dressing:
50ml white wine vinegar
125ml olive oil
125ml water
1/2 teaspoon coriander seeds, crushed
1/2 teaspoon white peppercorns, crushed
50g concentrated tomato purée
75ml lemon juice
10g garlic, peeled and crushed
1 small bouquet garni
50g caster sugar

Vegetables:
4 baby fennel bulbs, trimmed
4 baby courgettes, halved lengthways
24 French beans
8 radishes
8 small spring onions
8 small button mushrooms

Scrambled eggs:
60g butter
8 eggs
60ml double cream
salt and freshly ground pepper

To garnish:
4 bundles of 10–12 chives
2 tablespoons snipped chives

Put all the ingredients for the à la grecque dressing in a saucepan over a low heat, add salt and simmer gently for 20 minutes, stirring occasionally with a whisk.

Blanch all the vegetables except the mushrooms separately in boiling water: allow 2 minutes for the fennel; about 30 seconds for the courgettes, French beans, radishes and spring onions. Drain and add salt to taste.

Add all the vegetables to the dressing and simmer for 5 minutes. Discard the bouquet garni, tip the vegetables into a bowl and leave to cool at room temperature.

To prepare the scrambled eggs, melt the butter in a saucepan over a gentle heat. Break the eggs into a bowl, season with salt and pepper and beat lightly with a fork. Pour into the saucepan and cook over a very low heat, stirring gently and continuously with a wooden spoon until the eggs are scrambled and just cooked to your taste. Transfer them to a bowl, cover with cling film and cool at room temperature.

When the eggs are cold, whip the cream to a ribbon consistency and delicately fold into the eggs. Spoon them on to 4 serving plates. Using a slotted spoon, lift the vegetables from the dressing and arrange them around the eggs. Drizzle with a few drops of dressing. Garnish each plate with a bundle of chives and scatter the snipped chives over the scrambled eggs to serve.

scrambled eggs with crab

Cook the eggs as above until just scrambled to your liking. Take off the heat, add the whipped cream, then scatter 150g fresh white crab meat over the mixture. Mix gently and season to taste with salt and pepper. Divide between 4 warmed plates, and scatter 6–8 capers and a pinch of snipped chives over each serving. Serve at once.

POACHING EGGS

It is essential to use only very fresh eggs so that the whites completely cover the yolks. You can generally poach 4 eggs at a time. Three-quarters fill a shallow pan, about 5cm deep, with water and bring to the boil. Add 2 tablespoons white wine vinegar. Don't add salt to the water, or the egg whites will become pitted with tiny holes. Break an egg into a teacup and tip it very gently into the water at the point where it is bubbling. Add the other 3 eggs, one at a time, in this way and poach for about 2 minutes, according to how soft you like your eggs.

Use a small slotted spoon to lift out the first egg and press with your fingertip to check if it is properly cooked. If so, slip it into a bowl of iced water to prevent further cooking. Do the same with the other eggs.

Trim the eggs into a neat cushion shape. Hold the egg in your hand and pare off the untidy edges with a sharp knife (see below).

If you want to serve the eggs immediately, drain them on a tea-towel.

If you want to serve them later, leave them in the iced water in the fridge. To reheat the eggs, put them in an empty bowl, carefully cover with boiling water and leave for 15–20 seconds (not a moment longer, or they will go hard.) This way, you can even poach your eggs the day before for breakfast the next morning.

poached eggs on watercress salad with red pepper salsa

This is the simplest dish imaginable, but its refreshing taste and vibrant colours make it highly original.

Serves 4
4 slices of baguette, cut on the diagonal
240g tender watercress sprigs
4 tablespoons lemon and mint vinaigrette (page 17)
8 poached eggs (see left)
1/2 quantity red pepper salsa (page 22)
12 basil leaves
seeds from 1/2 pomegranate
salt and freshly ground pepper

Toast the baguette slices just before assembling the dish. Dress the watercress with the vinaigrette and arrange it in the middle of 4 serving plates. Lay a toasted baguette slice diagonally across the watercress. Season the eggs with salt and pepper, place on the toast and spoon on a little red pepper salsa.

Arrange 3 basil leaves on one side of each plate and spoon the rest of the salsa around them. Scatter a few pomegranate seeds over the watercress.

poached eggs with fondant white onions

Thinly slice 24 small white salad onions, and sweat in 80g butter over a low heat, until meltingly tender. Lightly brown 4 thin slices of baguette in clarified butter (page 188), spread with a little of the fondant onions, top with a poached egg, and cover thickly with the remaining onions. Sprinkle with snipped flat-leaf parsley and serve immediately.

tomato omelette

This is a tomato omelette as you have never seen one before. Slitting it open to reveal the vivid red filling makes for mouth-watering anticipation. It is also delicious served cold for an unusual summer lunch or picnic dish.

Serves 2

Filling:
250g tomatoes
1 tablespoon olive oil
1 garlic clove, peeled (optional)
a few basil leaves (optional)

Omelette:
5 eggs
2 tablespoons clarified butter (page 188)
salt and freshly ground pepper
thyme sprig, to garnish

To make the filling, skin, halve, deseed and dice the tomatoes. Heat the olive oil in a pan, add the tomatoes and cook gently for about 3 minutes, depending on how ripe they are. If you like, add the garlic at this stage and remove it when the tomatoes are cooked. Season lightly and keep on one side. Add the basil if you like.

To make the omelette, break the eggs into a bowl and season with salt and pepper. Add a spoonful of clarified butter and beat lightly with a fork.

Heat a frying pan (preferably non-stick), about 20cm in diameter, until very hot. Add the remaining butter and spread it over the surface of the pan. Quickly pour the eggs into the pan. Using the side of the fork so as not to scratch the surface of the pan,

keep stirring the eggs with one hand while shaking the pan with the other. When the omelette is set underneath, but still runny on top, spoon the tomato filling in a line along the middle.

Tilt and shake the pan away from you to push one half of the omelette towards the middle. Roll the omelette on to a serving plate.

With the tip of a knife, cut it lengthways down the middle to reveal the tomatoes (and add any leftover filling). Garnish with a sprig of thyme and brush the omelette with a touch of clarified butter to give it a sheen. Serve immediately.

variations

There is almost no limit to what you can put in an omelette. Some delicious fillings to add at the last moment, just before rolling the omelette, include:
- mussels *à la marinière*, either plain or tossed in a little garlicky butter.
- strips of smoked salmon which permeate the eggs to give a superb flavour.
- ratatouille made with tiny diced vegetables.
- for a substantial *omelette grand'mère*, bacon lardons fried with baby onions. Be creative!

eggah with grilled merguez

My interpretation of this rustic Moroccan dish reminds me of the time I spent in North Africa, and I often make it when I am at my house in the South of France.

Cook the eggah in a heatproof cast-iron, earthenware or porcelain dish, about 20cm in diameter and 4cm deep, and serve it straight from the dish. It is also good served cold for brunch; keep it in the larder or a cool place overnight, not in the fridge as this would deaden the flavours.

Serves 4

4 small merguez sausages
120g tomatoes
180g potatoes
4 tablespoons olive oil
2 garlic cloves, peeled and crushed
1/2 teaspoon harissa paste
8 eggs
1 teaspoon ground cumin
about 10 cardamom seeds
2 tablespoons snipped flat-leaf parsley
salt and freshly ground pepper

Preheat the oven to 180°C/gas mark 4. Heat a griddle pan until very hot, add the merguez sausages and turn to brown on all sides; they should be two-thirds cooked. Cut them in half, place on a plate and keep at room temperature.

Skin, deseed and dice the tomatoes. Peel and dice the potatoes. Heat 2 tablespoons olive oil in a non-stick frying pan and sauté the potatoes over a medium heat until golden and cooked. Add the garlic, cook for another 2–3 minutes, then put in the tomatoes and harissa. Cook gently for another 5 minutes.

Put the remaining oil in the heatproof dish and place on a heat diffuser over a medium heat.

Lightly beat the eggs with the cumin, cardamom seeds and a little salt and pepper.

When the oil is hot, add the egg mixture and cook, stirring with a fork, as if you were making an omelette, but over a lower heat. When the eggs are half-set, add the potato and tomato mixture and mix them delicately into the eggs, then push the merguez halfway into the eggah.

Cook in the oven for 6–8 minutes, depending how well you like your eggs cooked. Sprinkle with parsley and serve straight from the dish.

eggah with broad beans and tagliatelle

Serves 4
250g tagliatelle (preferably fresh, see page 84)
8 eggs
4 tablespoons olive oil
1 garlic clove, peeled and finely chopped
400g broad beans (weight in the pod), shelled, skinned and blanched
salt and freshly ground pepper

Preheat the oven to 180°C/gas mark 4. Cook the tagliatelle in boiling water until *al dente*; drain thoroughly and cut into 10cm lengths. Lightly beat the eggs with a little salt and pepper.

Heat the olive oil in a heatproof dish (preferably cast-iron), add the tagliatelle, and fry until lightly browned. Add the garlic, pour on the eggs, and cook as for eggah with grilled merguez (see above). Sprinkle on the broad beans, and cook in the oven for 4–6 minutes, until done to your liking. Serve very hot, straight from the dish.

parmesan and sorrel frittata

The freshness and acidity of sorrel counterbalances rich parmesan, and transforms this simple Italian frittata into a luscious lunch. Alternatively, you can cut it into diamonds and serve it as tapas.

Serves 4
70g butter
250g sorrel, stalks removed, and washed
12 eggs
2 tablespoons olive oil
100g parmesan, freshly grated
20g clarified butter (page 188)
salt and freshly ground pepper

Melt 30g butter in a small saucepan, add the sorrel, and wilt over a high heat for 1 minute. Immediately take off the heat, drain the sorrel and tip it into a bowl.

Beat the eggs in a bowl and season very lightly with salt and pepper. Heat the rest of the butter and the olive oil in a frying pan (preferably non-stick). When very hot, add the eggs, and cook as you would an omelette, stirring delicately every minute with the side of a fork until half-cooked.

Spread the sorrel over the surface, and sprinkle with parmesan, still stirring delicately with the fork. Lower the heat and cook until the frittata is set and pale golden underneath, then invert it on to a lightly buttered plate. Slide it back into the pan and cook on the other side for 2–3 minutes, until pale golden and done to your liking.

Slide the frittata on to a serving plate and brush the surface with a little clarified butter. Serve at once.

snail and herb frittata

Omit the sorrel and cheese. Pan-fry some snails in butter lightly flavoured with garlic. Meanwhile, half-cook the eggs as above. Scatter the pan-fried snails over the half-cooked eggs with a handful of snipped fresh herbs, and finish as above.

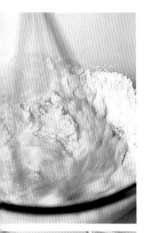

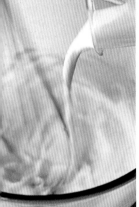

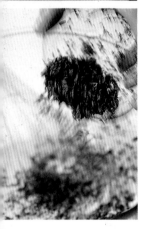

herb crêpes

These crêpes are so versatile. I use them in dishes, such as my wild mushroom and baby vegetable terrines (pages 76–7), and châteaubriand in a brioche crust (page 138). You can also fill them with savoury mixtures for an easy lunch or supper.

For an unusual dish, cook some merguez sausages on the barbecue, or fry over a high heat in a non-stick frying pan. At the last moment, brush herb crêpes with a little Dijon mustard, drizzle with maple syrup, and roll them round the sausages. This elegant way of serving merguez really brings out their flavour.

Makes six 26–30cm crêpes
60g plain flour
150ml milk
2 eggs
1 tablespoon chopped or snipped fresh herbs
salt and freshly ground pepper

For cooking:
1/2 small new potato
30g clarified butter (page 188)

Put the flour in a bowl and make a well in the middle. Add one-third of the milk, the eggs, a pinch of salt and a grinding of pepper. Mix lightly with a whisk to make a smooth batter, then stir in the rest of the milk. Cover with cling film and leave to rest for at least 30 minutes. Stir the herbs into the batter just before cooking.

To cook the crêpes, heat a 26–30cm frying pan. Spear the rounded side of the potato with a fork, dip into the clarified butter and slide the flat side over the hot pan surface to grease it; remove.

Stir the batter, then ladle just enough into the pan to cover the base. Cook quickly for about 1 minute, then toss the crêpe or turn it over with a palette knife and cook the other side for barely a minute. Make another 5 crêpes in the same way.

Stack the cooked crêpes on a plate, interleaving a band of greaseproof paper between each one to prevent them from sticking together.

seafood crêpes

Vary the seafood according to taste and availability using scallops instead of langoustines, or clams instead of mussels, for example. Laverbread has a surprisingly delicious iodine flavour. I think of it as the spice from the sea. (Illustrated on page 19.)

Serves 6
six 16–18cm herb crêpes (see left)
24 medium or large langoustines
100ml ml dry white wine
48 live mussels, cleaned
48 small button mushroom caps, wiped clean
30g butter
juice of 1 lemon
500ml sauce suprême, made with fish stock (page 18)
150g (2 pieces) laverbread seaweed (optional), rinsed
salt and freshly ground pepper
lemon wedges, to serve

Plunge the langoustines into a large pan of boiling salted water. As soon as it returns to the boil, turn off the heat, leave for 3 minutes, then drain. Cool, then shell and place in a bowl; cover with a damp cloth.

Put the wine in the pan and set over a high heat. Add the mussels, cover tightly and cook for 2–3 minutes, shaking the pan. As soon as they open, remove and drain, reserving the juice. Shell the mussels, place in a bowl and keep covered. Decant the liquid into a small pan, leaving behind any grit. Reduce over a medium heat to about 3 tablespoons; strain and reserve.

Put the mushrooms, butter and half the lemon juice in a pan. Barely cover with cold water, salt lightly and bring to the boil. Immediately turn off the heat; set aside.

Gently reheat the sauce suprême, stirring. Add the mussel liquid and cook gently for 5 minutes. Add the remaining lemon juice and check the seasoning.

Blanch the laverbread in boiling water for 1 minute. Drain and tear each piece into six. Add half to the sauce, with the mussels, langoustines and mushrooms. Heat gently for 5 minutes without boiling, stirring delicately from time to time.

Fill the warm crêpes with the seafood and sauce. Serve with lemon wedges and warm laverbread.

millefeuille of crêpes soufflées with redcurrants

This is yummy. It is best served as soon as it's assembled – you will need a long knife with a fine, sharp blade to cut it. It will be easier to cut if you place it in the freezer for 30 minutes or so before cutting, to firm up the filling. For an extra treat, serve the millefeuille with redcurrant and passion fruit coulis (page 28).

Serves 8

Crêpes soufflées:

75g plain flour
125ml milk
2 egg yolks
pinch of salt
20g caster sugar, plus a pinch
3 egg whites
50g clarified butter (page 188)

Filling:

100ml double cream
250ml crème pâtissière (page 181)
450g redcurrants, stalks removed

To decorate:

icing sugar to dust
few clusters of redcurrants

To assemble the millefeuille, you need a 15cm flan ring that is 5cm deep. Line it with a triple thick band of greaseproof paper that is 12cm deep (to extend above the ring) and secure with sticky tape.

To make the crêpe soufflée batter, put the flour into a bowl and make a well in the middle. Add two-thirds of the milk, the egg yolks, and a pinch each of salt and sugar. Mix gently with a balloon whisk until smooth, then stir in the remaining milk.

Beat the egg whites in a clean bowl until soft peaks form, then add the 20g sugar and beat until stiff. Gently fold into the crêpe soufflée batter.

Heat 10g clarified butter in a 15–20cm frying pan until very hot. Pour in one-fifth of the batter and tilt the pan to make a crêpe soufflé about 1.5cm thick. Cook for about 1¹/₂–2 minutes, until golden underneath, them carefully turn it over with a palette knife and cook the other side for about 1¹/₂ minutes. Place the crêpe soufflée on a sheet of greaseproof paper and cook another four in the same way. If necessary, trim the crêpes so that they will fit inside the prepared flan ring, using a sharp knife.

For the filling, whip the cream to soft peaks, then fold into the crème pâtissière. Spoon into a piping bag fitted with a 1.5–2cm plain nozzle.

Put the prepared flan ring on a serving plate and lay a crêpe inside, to make the base. Starting at the centre and working towards the edge, pipe a spiral of cream filling, about 1.5cm thick. Scatter over about a quarter of the redcurrants. Pipe a layer of cream on top as before, then cover with a second crêpe. Repeat the process three times, finishing with the fifth and final crêpe.

Refrigerate the millefeuille for up to 3 hours before serving, or pop it into the freezer for 30 minutes.

To serve, carefully remove the flan ring and paper in one deft movement. If necessary, smooth the edges with a palette knife. Dust with icing sugar and top with clusters of redcurrants. Serve right away.

chocolate crêpes

These crêpes are delectable served warm, with a coffee sabayon (page 31), whipped cream or vanilla ice cream. They also feature in my peppermint soufflé in a chocolate crêpe (page 64).

Makes twelve 14–16cm crêpes
125g plain flour
30g cocoa powder
400ml milk
2 eggs
50g caster sugar
pinch of salt
100ml double cream

For cooking:
¹/₂ small new potato
30g clarified butter (page 188)

Sift the flour and cocoa together into a bowl and make a well. Pour in one-third of the milk, break in the eggs and add the sugar and salt. Mix gently with a whisk to make a smooth batter, then stir in the cream and the rest of the milk. Pass through a sieve into a bowl. Cover with cling film and rest for at least 30 minutes.

To cook the crêpes, heat a 14–16cm frying pan. Spear the rounded side of the potato with a fork, dip into the clarified butter and slide over the surface of the hot pan to grease it; remove.

Stir the batter, then ladle just enough into the pan to cover the base. Cook quickly for about 1 minute, then toss the crêpe or turn it over with a palette knife and cook on the other side for barely a minute. Cook all the crêpes in the same way and stack them on a plate, interleaving with greaseproof paper to prevent them from sticking together. Serve warm.

smoked haddock soufflé with poached egg "en surprise"

This soufflé has featured on the winter menu at The Waterside Inn for many years. Our regular customers never tire of it; the mingling of the runny yolk – from the hidden poached egg – with the smoked haddock is a source of delight.

Serves 4

Béchamel:
25g butter, softened
25g flour
400ml milk

Soufflé:
6 egg yolks
40g butter, softened
140g gruyère, finely grated
120g smoked haddock fillet
400ml double cream
8 egg whites (ie 280g)
1 tablespoon snipped dill
4 poached eggs (page 54)
salt and freshly ground pepper

Garnish:
4 poached quail's eggs
4 dill sprigs

Preheat the oven to 220°C/gas mark 7. To make the béchamel, melt the butter in a small heavy-based saucepan. Off the heat, stir in the flour, then return the pan to a low heat and cook for 3 minutes, stirring continuously with a small whisk. Off the heat, pour in the milk, stirring. Place on a medium heat and bring to the boil, stirring all the time. Lower the heat and simmer for about 10 minutes, still stirring continuously.

Off the heat, mix the 6 egg yolks into the béchamel and season with salt and pepper. Cover this soufflé base with cling film and set aside at room temperature.

Grease the insides of 4 individual 10cm soufflé dishes, 6.5cm deep, with softened butter. Sprinkle a small handful of grated gruyère into one soufflé dish, rotate it to coat the inside, then tip the excess into a second dish. Repeat the process to coat all 4 dishes.

Put the smoked haddock into a small saucepan, pour on the cream and place over a low heat. When the cream starts bubbling, reduce the heat to a gentle simmer and cook for 5 minutes. Turn off the heat and leave until cool enough to handle, then remove the skin and flake the fish with your fingertips, removing any small bones. Leave the fish in the cream.

In a clean bowl, beat the egg whites with a pinch of salt to soft peaks. Whisk one-third of the egg whites into the soufflé base to loosen it.

Add this mixture to the remaining egg whites and fold in delicately, using a spatula, adding the gruyère and dill as you go.

At this point, cover the poached eggs with boiling water for 15 seconds to warm them, then drain on kitchen paper.

Half-fill each prepared dish with the soufflé mixture, then spoon in the creamy haddock mix.

Put a poached egg in the middle and fill the dishes with the remaining soufflé mixture to come slightly above the top. Smooth the surface with a palette knife.

Run a knife around the edge of the mixture to ease it away from the side of the dish; this helps the soufflé to rise. Stand the soufflé dishes in a roasting pan and pour in enough boiling water to come halfway up the sides. Cook in the oven for 6 minutes.

Top each soufflé with a quail's egg and a sprig of dill, and serve immediately.

grand marnier and mango soufflés

Sometimes I top these individual sweet soufflés with a few very thin strands of orange zest lightly poached in sugar syrup, or a spoonful of passion fruit seeds. The sharp piquancy adds an elusive quality to their delicacy and lightness.

Serves 4

30g butter, softened
170g caster sugar
250ml milk
1 vanilla pod, split lengthways
3 egg yolks
25g potato flour
105ml Grand Marnier
100g very ripe mango flesh, cut into small pieces
7 egg whites (ie 245g)
icing sugar, to dust

Brush the inside of 4 individual 10cm soufflé dishes, 4cm deep, with softened butter. Put 30g sugar in one of the dishes, and rotate it to coat the inside thoroughly. Tip the excess sugar into the next dish, and repeat to coat them all with sugar. Put a baking sheet in the oven and preheat to 180°C/gas mark 4.

Pour the milk into a small heavy-based pan. Scrape the seeds from the vanilla pod and add them to the milk with the pod and 20g sugar. Bring to the boil.

Put the egg yolks and 10g sugar in a bowl, and whisk to a ribbon consistency. Add the potato flour, and whisk thoroughly until very smooth. Pour the boiling milk on to the egg mixture, whisking as you go, then return the mixture to the saucepan. Bubble over a low heat for 2 minutes, whisking continuously. Take off the heat, remove the vanilla pod, then add 75ml Grand Marnier. Tip the pastry cream into a bowl and set aside.

Melt 30g sugar in a non-stick, heavy-based saucepan over a low heat and cook to a pale, nut-brown caramel. Add the mango pieces and brown them in the caramel for 1 minute. Add the remaining 2 tablespoons Grand Marnier and cook for another minute. Set aside.

To assemble the soufflés, beat the egg whites to soft peaks. Add the remaining 80g sugar and continue to beat until the meringue is firm, but not too stiff. Using a balloon whisk, mix one-third into the pastry cream, then delicately fold in the rest with a spatula.

Divide half the soufflé mixture between the dishes. Spoon in the mango, then fill up the dishes with the rest of the mixture. Smooth the surface with a palette knife, and lightly draw the mixture away from the edge of the dishes with the tip of a small knife. Immediately, place the dishes on the hot baking sheet and bake for about 8 minutes.

To serve, dust the soufflés with a light veil of icing sugar and serve right away, or place them under a hot grill or salamander for 30 seconds until glazed and caramelised, then serve immediately.

peppermint soufflé in a chocolate crêpe

This flavour combination of dark, bitter chocolate and peppermint liqueur is a chocoholic's delight.

Serves 6
150g crème pâtissière (page 181)
30ml peppermint liqueur (eg crème de menthe)
4 egg whites (ie 140g)
40g caster sugar
50g good quality dark, bitter chocolate, chopped
6 chocolate crêpes (page 61)

To serve:
6 mint sprigs
icing sugar to dust

Preheat the oven to 200°C/gas mark 6. Put the crème pâtissière into a bowl and heat gently in a bain-marie or the microwave. Stir in the peppermint liqueur.

Beat the egg whites until soft peaks form, then add the sugar and beat to stiff peaks. Using a whisk, mix a third of the meringue into the flavoured crème pâtissière to loosen it. Delicately fold in the rest of the meringue, using a spatula. Scatter the chocolate over the surface and mix in gently.

Lay the crêpes on a large baking sheet. Working quickly and delicately, use a large spoon to pile the soufflé mixture into a dome in the middle of each crêpe. Fold the crêpes over the filling to enclose and immediately place in the hot oven for 3–4 minutes.

Take the crêpes out of the oven and lift them on to serving plates with a palette knife. Add the mint sprigs, sprinkle the crêpes with icing sugar and serve at once.

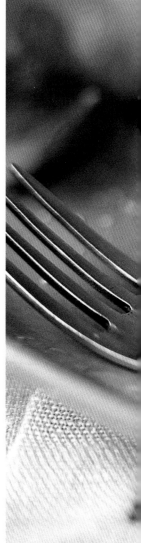

mousses, terrines and confits

Mousses and confits require little effort and are relatively easy to prepare. Terrines, however, take time and a degree of organisation ... and there are no short cuts. Don't let this discourage you, as these rustic dishes keep well for several days in the fridge and their pleasure can extend across several meals. A combination of mousses and terrines is perfect for a buffet, or as an hors d'oeuvre. They give the host a breather before the meal, leaving more time to devote attention to the main dish.

I use mainly seasonal ingredients, so my wild mushroom terrine (page 76), for example, only features on my menus in autumn, when several varieties of wild mushroom are available. It is important to get the seasoning just right, otherwise the flavour will be disappointing; taste the separate components as you assemble a terrine.

Being the son and grandson of a charcutier, confits hold no secrets for me. They are popular in France, especially in the country areas of the south and south-west. Slow-cooked dishes, like *potées* of green cabbage, sarladaise potatoes and cassoulets benefit from the addition of confit goose, duck or pork. I never shun them, and I am particularly fond of my original creation of confit rabbit, which I prepare mainly in winter to grill and serve with a salad.

Of the many tempting mousses based on puréed cooked meat or vegetables, ham mousse (page 69) is one of my favourites. In winter, I often prepare delicate fish or chicken mousses to serve hot, as in my salmon mousse and spinach tartlets (page 70). I sometimes shape these mousses into quenelles, using two tablespoons (see page 69), then poach them in lightly salted water. Creamy and light, they can be coated with hollandaise sauce to make them even more delectable.

The aroma of an eye-catching terrine will make your mouth water, and these appetising dishes are wonderfully versatile. Vary the lining to suit the different flavours and colours in the terrine; thin strips of back fat, pig's caul, thin crêpes, finely sliced courgettes, blanched leek and green cabbage leaves are all suitable. Terrines can be assembled from pork or veal forcemeat, chicken, game, offal, mousses or small pieces of fish; the possible varieties of colour and texture are endless.

More and more, I am enjoying confit vegetables, such as peppers, aubergines, courgettes and tomatoes. These have a delicate texture, and should be served as soon as they are ready. I also confit pieces of fish, like chunks of eel or thick salmon fillets, which melt in the mouth.

For fish and meat, I only use fats of the purest quality, taken from the bellies of ducks and geese. These fine fats, available commercially in jars, help to develop the flavours of the main ingredients. For vegetables, I use light olive oil or groundnut oil, or clarified butter. Like a court-bouillon, the fat or oil should be flavoured with a bouquet garni, some crushed peppercorns and unpeeled garlic cloves; but don't add salt, as the meat and fish will have already been salted.

I keep confit meats in their fat in the fridge for weeks, so I always have a quick meal on hand – perfect for the holidays or when friends turn up unexpectedly. I can relax, and entertain them with a smile ...

ham mousse with red pepper salsa

This simple, tasty mousse is rustic yet sophisticated – a real gourmet dish. I prefer the texture to be slightly rough, but if you like a creamier mousse, rub it through a fine sieve before mixing in the cream. For the best flavour, use a good quality unsmoked ham, cooked on the bone. Prepare the ham mousse a day or two in advance if you like – shape it into quenelles and arrange on the plates 20 minutes before serving.

Serves 8

3 gelatine leaves
350ml velouté sauce made with chicken stock (page 18)
1/2 teaspoon paprika
800ml whipping cream
350g good quality unsmoked cooked ham, diced
pinch of cayenne pepper
50ml dry sherry
salt and freshly ground pepper

To serve:

16 small asparagus spears
handful of radicchio and mâche (lamb's lettuce)
few drops of lemon juice, to taste
24 hazelnuts, toasted, skinned and halved
red pepper salsa (page 22)

Soften the gelatine leaves in cold water to cover. Slowly heat the velouté sauce until it just reaches a simmer, then take the pan off the heat. Thoroughly drain the gelatine leaves and add them to the sauce, together with the paprika. Whisk thoroughly until the gelatine has melted. Leave to cool at room temperature, stirring with a whisk from time to time.

Whip the cream to a ribbon consistency. Put the diced ham into a food processor and whizz for 1 minute, then add the velouté and process for 2–3 minutes to make a smooth paste. Transfer to a bowl and place over another bowl containing ice cubes to chill the mixture.

Gently fold the whipped cream into the mixture, with a spatula. Season with salt and cayenne, then gently mix in the sherry; avoid overworking the mousse. Taste and adjust the seasoning with pepper.

Scrape the mousse into a dish, cover the surface with cling film to prevent oxidisation (which would turn the mousse grey), then refrigerate.

Take the ham mousse out of the fridge 20 minutes before serving. Peel the ends of the asparagus spears, halve lengthways and blanch lightly; drain thoroughly. Dress the radicchio and mâche, simply, with a few drops of lemon juice.

Shape the mousse into quenelles (see below), allowing one or two per person, and place on serving plates. Arrange the radicchio and mâche, asparagus and toasted hazelnuts on the plates. Spoon a little red pepper salsa over the ham mousse and accompany with toasted country bread.

SHAPING QUENELLES

Dip two tablespoons into a bowl of warm water to warm them. Scrape one spoon through the mousse towards you to take up an oval quenelle (left). Mould the quenelle onto the second spoon (centre), then back onto the first spoon (right) to improve the shape. Place the quenelle on the serving plate.

salmon mousse and spinach tartlets

This simple, yet sophisticated starter is full of wonderful flavours. With the exception of the hollandaise, all the components can be prepared in advance, including the salmon mousse gnocchi. Make the hollandaise just before the meal and serve the extra sauce in a sauceboat.

Serves 6

Tartlet cases:
360g pâte brisée (page 174)
flour, to dust

Salmon mousse:
250g salmon fillet, skinned
1 egg white
small pinch of cayenne pepper
350ml double cream, well chilled
salt

To assemble:
60g butter
300g small spinach leaves, washed and stalks removed
pinch of sugar
6 small dill or fennel fronds, plus extra for garnish
1 quantity hollandaise sauce (page 20)

First make the tartlet cases: Lightly flour the work surface and roll out the pastry thinly, to a 2–3mm thickness. Cut out six 10cm circles with a pastry cutter and use them to line six 8cm tartlet tins. Trim off the excess pastry with a small sharp knife. Place the tartlet cases in the fridge and leave to rest for about 20 minutes. Preheat the oven to 200°C/gas mark 6.

Prick the tartlet bases with a fork, line with a disc of greaseproof paper or foil, and fill with dried or ceramic baking beans. Bake for 8 minutes, then remove the beans and paper or foil. Bake for another 2 minutes. Unmould the pastry cases and place on a wire rack.

To prepare the mousse, put the salmon in a food processor and whizz to a smooth purée. Rub the salmon purée through a fine sieve into a bowl placed on a bed of crushed ice. Using a spatula, gradually work the egg white into the purée, then season with the cayenne and a little salt. Add the cream, little by little, working it in with the spatula, until you have a slightly firm mousse. Cover the bowl with cling film and refrigerate until ready to use.

Two-thirds fill a shallow 20cm saucepan with lightly salted water. Bring to the boil and reduce the heat so that the water is barely trembling.

To shape the gnocchi, spoon the mousse into a piping bag fitted with a 1cm plain nozzle. Twist the end to secure and using one hand, hold the piping bag 5cm above the water. Hold a knife in the other hand.

Apply a consistent, slow pressure to squeeze the mousse from the bag, at the same time stroking the back of the blade over the end of the nozzle, to cut the emerging mousse into 1cm lengths; allow them to drop into the water. Continue until you have cut half the mousse into gnocchi. Poach them in the barely simmering water for about 2 minutes; they will bob up to the surface when they are cooked.

Using a slotted spoon, transfer them to a bowl of iced water and leave to cool completely. Prepare and cook the remaining gnocchi in the same way.

Heat the oven to 160°C/gas mark 3. Melt the butter in a frying pan over a medium heat. Increase the heat to high, add the spinach with the sugar, and sauté briefly. Season lightly with salt and drain well. Keep warm.

To assemble, warm the pastry cases in the oven for a few minutes. Divide the spinach between them. Plunge the gnocchi into a pan of boiling water for 1 minute to heat them, drain and carefully pile into the pastry cases. Shred the dill or fennel over the gnocchi and coat with hollandaise. Garnish with fennel or dill and serve.

wild boar and morel pâté en croûte

A pear and lime salsa is the perfect foil for this wonderful pâté, which is equally good made with organic pork or pheasant. It will keep in the fridge for up to 5 days.

Serves 8

I boned shoulder of wild boar (about 500g), trimmed of fat and sinews, bones and trimmings reserved
150g veal fillet
200g pork fat
2 tablespoons groundnut oil
2 carrots, peeled and chopped
1 onion, peeled and chopped
100ml dry white wine
1 bouquet garni
3 gelatine leaves, soaked in cold water
200ml double cream
1/2 egg, beaten
pinch of cayenne pepper
300g pâte brisée (page 174)
flour, to dust
200g back fat, finely sliced
40g dried morels, soaked in cold water
fine sea salt and freshly ground pepper
1 egg yolk, mixed with 1 tablespoon milk (eggwash)

To serve:

pear and lime salsa (page 23)
pickled baby beetroot (page 188), optional
pickled damsons (page 188), optional

Cut the wild boar, veal and pork fat into cubes and chill until almost frozen. Meanwhile, make the jelly. Chop the bones. Heat the oil in a frying pan, add the bones, trimmings and sinews and fry until lightly coloured. Add the carrots and onion, fry for 3 minutes, then tip everything into a saucepan. Deglaze the frying pan with the white wine and add to the saucepan. Add cold water to cover the bones generously and bring to the boil. Reduce the heat, add the bouquet garni and simmer gently for 1 1/2 hours, skimming as necessary.

Strain the stock through a muslin-lined sieve, slowly so that it remains clear. Squeeze out the water from the gelatine leaves, add them to the stock and stir until melted. Season with salt and leave until cool and slightly thickened.

To prepare the forcemeat, pass the wild boar, veal and pork fat through the coarse blade of a mincer. Mix in the cream, beaten egg, 1 1/2 teaspoons salt, 1/2 teaspoon pepper, and the cayenne, with a spatula.

Roll out the pastry on a lightly floured surface to a 50cm square, 5mm thick. Lay the back fat on the pastry, leaving a 5cm clear border all round. Spread a 2cm layer of forcemeat over the middle third of the fat. Top with a few morels and cover with another layer of forcemeat. Repeat these layers to use all the forcemeat and morels. Completely enclose the forcemeat with back fat by folding over the overhanging pieces.

Lightly brush the short ends of the pastry with eggwash. Fold one long side over the forcemeat, brush with eggwash, then fold the other long side over the top. Roll out the pastry ends and trim to make 8cm flaps. Brush lightly with eggwash and fold them up over the pâté. Hold a baking sheet at an angle of 45° against the side of the pâté, then tilt and invert the pâté on to the baking sheet. Refrigerate for 1 hour.

Preheat the oven to 200°C/gas mark 6. Brush the pastry all over with eggwash and lightly score leaves or a lattice pattern with a knife tip. Make two small openings with a knife tip to let steam escape, then cook in the oven for 10 minutes.

Reduce the setting to 180°C/gas mark 4 and cook for a further 50 minutes, or until a trussing needle or fine knife tip inserted into the centre of the pâté for 10 seconds is hot when withdrawn. If the pastry seems to be over-browning during cooking, cover it with foil.

Using a palette knife, move the pâté to a cooling rack and leave for 2 hours or until cold. Insert a small funnel in each opening and pour in the slightly thickened jelly. Refrigerate for 24 hours.

To serve, cut the pâté into slices, with a sharp knife; discard the ends. Put a slice of pâté on each plate and add a spoonful of pear and lime salsa. Accompany with pickled beetroot and damsons if you like.

wild mushroom terrine

The earthy forest flavours in this terrine are quite astonishing. Depending on availability and cost, you can make the terrine with only two or three varieties of mushroom. It will lose some of its visual impact, but the flavour will still be superb. Use a rectangular dish, approximately 20x6x6cm. This terrine keeps well in the fridge for up to 4 to 5 days.

For vegetarians, use vegetable rather than chicken stock, increasing the gelatine by one third.

Serves 8–10

500g ceps (preferably small ones)
750g golden chanterelles or girolles
250g trompettes de la mort (horns of plenty)
250g oyster mushrooms
125g enoki mushrooms
1.5 litres chicken stock (page 16) or vegetable stock (page 17)
150g chicken breast fillets, finely chopped
3 egg whites
40g leek, finely sliced
40g celery, finely sliced
40g carrot, peeled and cut into thin rings
8 (or more) gelatine leaves
4 herb crêpes (page 58), 26–30 cm diameter
salt and freshly ground white pepper

To serve:

dandelion leaves, or other peppery salad leaves
tarragon leaves
few perfect, small golden chanterelles or girolles, tossed in a light vinaigrette

Using a small knife, cut off the base of the mushrooms and remove any earth, sand or damaged parts. Halve the trompettes down the middle and check to make sure they are free of sand and grit. Carefully and briefly wash the different mushrooms separately in cold water, then drain well; the enoki won't need washing.

Bring the stock to the boil in a saucepan and cook the different mushrooms, one variety at a time. Allow 5 minutes for ceps; 4 minutes for chanterelles or girolles; 2 minutes each for trompettes de la mort and oyster mushrooms; 30 seconds for enoki. As soon as they are cooked, lift them out with a slotted spoon and drain in a colander. When all the mushrooms are cooked, boil the stock to reduce it by one third. Leave the mushrooms and stock to cool.

Set the ceps aside, then gently press the rest of the mushrooms, mix together and refrigerate.

To clarify the reduced stock, put the chicken, egg whites and vegetables in a saucepan, mix with a whisk and tip in the cold stock. Bring the mixture to the boil, stirring continuously with the whisk, then turn the heat to very low and simmer gently for 30 minutes. Strain the stock through a fine chinois or muslin-lined sieve into a bowl and measure the quantity.

Allow 8 gelatine leaves per 500ml stock. Soften in cold water, then squeeze out excess water and add to the stock, stirring gently with a spoon. Leave until cold, then season generously.

To assemble, line the terrine with cling film, letting it overhang the top edge. Trim the crêpes into squares and arrange side-by-side on the cling film to line the dish, leaving plenty of overhang at both ends and one side. Pour in half the cold, liquid jelly, scatter in half the mixed mushrooms (but not the ceps) and press down gently to embed them in the jelly; they should half-fill the dish. Refrigerate until the jelly begins to set.

Lay the ceps in a line along the middle of the terrine, then gently pour in the rest of the liquid jelly to 2cm from the top. Scatter in the remaining mushrooms and push them lightly into the jelly. Fold the overhanging crêpes over the terrine to enclose it, then fold the cling film over the top; refrigerate for at least 24 hours.

To serve, invert the terrine on to a board, unmould, then carefully peel off the cling film. Using a long, fine-bladed knife dipped in warm water, cut the terrine into 1.5–2cm thick slices. Lay a slice on each plate, arrange a few dandelion leaves on one side and strew with tarragon leaves. Arrange the chanterelles alongside.

terrine of baby vegetables

The tiny vegetables in this delicate, flavoursome terrine make it so appealing. Serve it cold, or warm with a pear and lime salsa (page 23) or a drizzle of olive oil. Simply slice the terrine and steam for a few minutes to warm through. You will need a rectangular mould about 20x6x6cm.

Serves 8–10

Celeriac mousse:

1/2 celeriac, about 300g
500ml double cream
4 eggs
3 egg yolks
salt and freshly ground white pepper

Baby vegetables:

125g baby artichokes (the kind you can eat raw)
50ml dry white wine
2 tablespoons olive oil
juice of 1 lemon
150g baby carrots, peeled
175g baby fennel
150g medium asparagus spears
125g baby courgettes
125g broccoli florets
4 herb crêpes (page 58), 26–30cm diameter

Garnish:

confit tomatoes (page 79)
samphire
caperberries
fennel fronds

First make the celeriac mousse. Peel the celeriac and cut into 2cm pieces. Place in a saucepan with the cream and cook gently for about 30 minutes, stirring occasionally, until the celeriac is tender and the cream has reduced by half. Tip into a food processor and whizz for 3 minutes, or until smooth. Leave in the processor to cool slightly, until warm. Add the whole eggs, egg yolks and seasoning and whizz for 1 minute. Turn into a bowl, cover with cling film and set aside at room temperature.

To prepare the artichokes, cut off the tips of the leaves with a knife and pare the base to leave only the tender part of the stem and heart. Put the artichokes in a saucepan with the white wine, olive oil, lemon juice, and enough water to cover. Cook over a low heat for about 8 minutes until the artichokes are tender and soft. Leave to cool in the liquid, then drain and pat dry; set aside.

Peel, trim and wash all the other vegetables. Lightly cook them separately in boiling salted water until *al dente*. Plunge into iced water, drain and pat dry.

Preheat the oven to 160°C/gas mark 3. To assemble the terrine, line the mould with cling film, letting it overhang all round. Use a knife to trim the crêpes into squares and arrange them side-by-side on the cling film, leaving plenty of overhang at both ends and one side of the mould.

Spread a 2–3cm layer of cold celeriac mousse over the base. Arrange a line of one variety of vegetable over the mousse and cover with more mousse. Gently tap the terrine to settle it and layer the other vegetables and remaining mousse in the same way, finishing with a 3cm layer of mousse. Fold the overhanging crêpes, then the cling film over the top. Stand the terrine in a bain-marie and cook in the oven for about 1¹/₄ hours. To check if it is cooked, push a trussing needle or fine skewer into the centre for 10 seconds; it should come out completely clean and feel hot. Leave the terrine to cool, then refrigerate for at least 24 hours before serving.

To serve, invert the terrine on to a board, unmould and carefully peel off the cling film. Using a fine-bladed knife dipped into warm water, cut into 1.5–2cm slices. Place on individual plates and garnish with confit tomatoes, some samphire, a few caperberries, some fennel fronds and a coarse grinding of white pepper.

confit tomatoes

Confit vegetables are wonderfully versatile. You can serve them alone as tapas, or with toasted country bread, in pasta dishes, salads or as hors d'oeuvres. To serve them warm, simply heat under a medium grill or in a saucepan, with a splash of their preserving oil. They can be kept in their oil in the fridge for up to 2 weeks.

Light olive oil is the ideal medium for confit vegetables. Note that olive oil should always be stored away from direct light and used soon after opening, otherwise its flavour is liable to alter and deteriorate.

Confit tomatoes feature in my grilled fillet of lamb with Mediterranean vegetables (page 116).

Makes about 1kg

1kg very ripe tomatoes (eg Roma or Marmande), on the vine if possible
1 litre olive oil
2 thyme sprigs
1 bay leaf
2 garlic cloves, peeled and halved
1 teaspoon white peppercorns, crushed
salt

Peel the tomatoes, halve or quarter them, and remove the seeds. Heat the oil in a saucepan until very hot but not smoking, then throw in the tomatoes, thyme, bay leaf, garlic and pepper. Lower the heat and cook gently at about 70°C for 15–20 minutes, depending on how ripe the tomatoes are.

Leave to cool in the pan, then transfer the tomatoes to a jar. Pour in enough oil to cover them, seal the jar with cling film and refrigerate until needed. Remove the tomatoes from the oil and season with salt to taste just before serving.

confit sweet peppers

These peppers taste superb if they are grilled on a barbecue. If available, I add some vine shoots to enhance the flavour.

Makes about 600g

500g red, yellow or green peppers
600ml olive oil
2 thyme sprigs
1 bay leaf
1 rosemary sprig
1 garlic clove
1 teaspoon white peppercorns, crushed

Using your fingertips, oil the peppers very lightly with a little of the olive oil. Grill under a very high heat (or barbecue for the best flavour), turning them until the skin blisters and blackens all over.

When the peppers are almost burnt, plunge them into a bowl of iced water, then remove and peel them. Halve the peppers lengthways and remove the white membrane and seeds. Leave them as they are, or cut each half into two.

Heat the oil in a saucepan until very hot but not smoking. Add the peppers, thyme, bay leaf, rosemary, garlic and peppercorns. Cook gently at about 70°C for approximately 30 minutes.

Leave the peppers to cool in the saucepan, then transfer them to a jar or bowl. Pour in enough oil to cover them, seal the jar with cling film and keep in the fridge until ready to use.

confit garlic

Use these sweet garlic cloves as a garnish for roast or grilled chicken and lamb, toss into cooked pasta, or smear on warm toast and sprinkle with pepper.

Makes about 600g

500g new season's garlic
500ml olive oil
1 rosemary sprig
1 bay leaf
1 teaspoon coriander seeds

Peel the garlic, or leave unpeeled if you prefer. Heat the oil in a saucepan until very hot but not smoking, then add the other ingredients. Cook gently at about 70°C for 10 minutes if the garlic is peeled, 15 minutes if not.

Leave the garlic to cool in the saucepan, then transfer it to a jar. Pour in enough olive oil to cover, then cover the jar with cling film and refrigerate until ready to use.

rabbit confit

I prepare confits with all kinds of meat and poultry, from duck legs to pieces of pork shoulder, neck of lamb, poultry gizzards, whole quail and pigeon. The method is always the same. You just need to adjust the salting and cooking times according to the size of the ingredient.

It is always handy to have a confit in the fridge, ready to grill or roast (depending on the variety) for impromptu entertaining. I often serve a confit with shredded cavolo nero, stir-fried until crunchy and scattered over lentils. The combination of crisp cabbage, tender lentils and rich confit is sheer perfection. And do try my grilled confit of rabbit with apples and walnuts (page 123), illustrated opposite.

Serves 4

4 rabbit legs
4 rabbit shoulders
100g coarse cooking salt
4 thyme sprigs
2 bay leaves
1.5kg duck fat or olive oil
10g crushed white peppercorns, 1 thyme sprig and 2 bay leaves, tied in a piece of muslin

Using your fingertips, rub the salt firmly into the rabbit legs for about 3 minutes and the shoulders for about 2 minutes. Closely pack all the rabbit pieces into a deep dish, adding the thyme sprigs and bay leaves. Cover with cling film and refrigerate for 30 minutes, then take out the shoulders, leaving the legs for another 15 minutes. Rinse the shoulders under a trickle of cold water and pat them dry with a tea-towel. Do the same with the legs.

Heat the duck fat or olive oil to 70°C in a flameproof casserole or roasting pan and add the muslin bag of herbs and peppercorns. Plunge in the rabbit legs and cook for 15 minutes, then add the shoulders. Cook for another 30 minutes, keeping the temperature at a constant 70°C. Turn off the heat and leave the rabbit to cool in the fat or oil at room temperature for at least 2 hours.

Using kitchen tongs or a fork, carefully transfer the rabbit pieces to a bowl or deep dish. Strain the cooking fat or oil through a chinois on to the rabbit pieces. Cover with cling film and refrigerate.

This confit will keep in the fridge for a couple of weeks. It can be served either roasted or grilled. Simply remove the fat from the rabbit pieces before you cook them.

pasta, grains and rice

Pasta has been part of my repertoire ever since I began cooking. I love making ravioli filled with tender vegetables, ricotta and sultanas; fish and seafood (notably lobster); chicken mousse or meat. To ring the changes, I flavour and colour the pasta, and make cappelletti. I fill these with wild mushrooms and serve them with herb salsa (page 88), or a purée of Jerusalem artichokes or carrots with coriander. In autumn, I tint the pasta red with beetroot juice; in winter, I use black squid or cuttlefish ink; in summer, yellow saffron infused in water;

Basmati rice must be soaked in cold water for 20 minutes before using; this helps it to absorb the cooking water. Basmati is a good balance for spicy dishes, as its neutral taste absorbs the flavours. It is delicious cooked with a touch of grated fresh ginger and lemon grass.

I like to use carnaroli rice for my seafood risotto with crustacean essence (page 94). A risotto is like a soufflé – it won't wait for your guests, so they must wait for it. Round-grain arborio rice makes a good creamy rice pudding, to serve with poached cherries (page 106).

Whatever the dish, note that it is not wise to reheat rice, as this can activate a harmful bacteria, *bacillus cereus,* which is sometimes present in all varieties. If you must reheat rice, then do so shortly after cooking and make sure that it is boiling hot.

and in spring, I layer flat-leaf parsley, basil, tarragon or fennel fronds between two thin sheets of pasta to give a delicate green, herb-flavoured marbling – a reflection of nature on the plate.

When entertaining on a large scale, I cook my pasta *al dente* beforehand, refresh, drain and toss it in a little groundnut oil, then spread it on a plate, cover with cling film and refrigerate. When ready to serve, I reheat it in boiling water for 30 seconds, drain, and toss it in melted butter or olive oil. Pasta is equally delicious served cold with a salsa or vinaigrette, or mixed with a little mayonnaise (page 20).

The best rice I have tasted on my travels has been in Vietnam and Italy. I use varieties from all over the world, choosing them to complement my recipes. Thai jasmine rice must be rinsed in cold water before cooking; I then fold it in a muslin cloth and cook it in a steamer for 30 minutes, stirring with a kitchen fork every 10 minutes to aerate it.

I often serve grain-based dishes – such as couscous, polenta and tabbouleh – on their own, enhancing their flavour and appearance with delicate ingredients like fresh herbs, grated cheese, seafood and baby vegetables. For a couscous *garni* (which I like very spicy), I vary the meats and vegetables according to the season. As it is an abundant dish, I never serve a first course beforehand; just a light, refreshing lime-scented mint sorbet afterwards.

In summer, I mix my tabbouleh with cold lobster or langoustine tails and confit tomatoes; redolent with lemon and parsley, this refreshing dish has a strong Mediterranean influence.

In winter, I cook polenta in hot chicken stock or milk to a soft purée consistency, then off the heat, I add egg yolks, grated parmesan and sautéed sliced ceps. When cold, I form it into cakes, fry these in a little olive oil and serve with roast or pan-fried pheasant ... delicious!

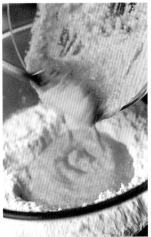

pasta dough

This recipe is meant for 4 people, but no doubt some will find it just enough for one. The dough is very malleable and is perfect for cappelletti, ravioli, and all filled pasta. You can make it in a food processor, but you must be careful to avoid overworking the mixture.

Serves 4
3 egg yolks
1¹/₂ whole eggs
2 teaspoons olive oil
2 teaspoons cold water
¹/₂ teaspoon fine salt
250g Italian "tipo 00" flour

Put all the ingredients, except the flour, in a bowl and mix lightly with a fork.

Tip the flour into a large bowl, make a well in the middle and add the liquid mixture. Use the fingertips of one hand to mix the wet ingredients, gradually drawing in the flour with the other hand, until it is all incorporated and you have a homogeneous dough.

Turn the dough on to a floured surface and sprinkle with flour. Knead and stretch the dough 3 or 4 times with the palm of your hand until it is pliable. Roll it into a ball, wrap in cling film and leave to rest in the fridge for 1 hour.

green olive pasta

The taste of green olives in this unusual pasta is so pleasant that I always serve myself a very generous portion, which I sauce with just a drizzle of extra virgin olive oil. The dough is softer than the plain version and cooks very quickly, so it will be perfectly *al dente* in just a few minutes.

Serves 6
1 whole egg
2 egg yolks
2 teaspoons olive oil
100g green olives, pitted, patted dry and very finely chopped
¹/₂ teaspoon fine salt
300g Italian "tipo 00" flour

Put the egg, egg yolks, olive oil, olives and salt in a bowl and mix lightly with a fork.

Tip the flour into a large bowl, make a well in the middle and add the olive mixture. Use the fingertips of one hand to mix the wet ingredients, gradually drawing in the flour with the other hand, until it is all incorporated and you have a homogeneous dough.

Turn the dough on to a floured surface and sprinkle with flour. Knead and stretch the dough 3 or 4 times with the palm of your hand, then roll it into a ball. Wrap in cling film and leave to rest in the fridge for 1 hour.

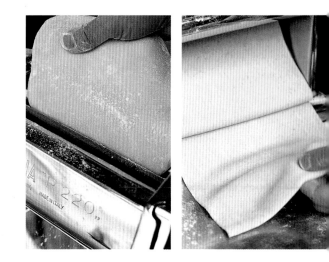

ROLLING AND SHAPING PASTA

Roll out the dough in manageable quantities, keeping the rest wrapped in cling film to stop it drying out. Pass it through the pasta machine on the widest setting, then repeatedly reducing the setting by one notch each time, until the pasta is about 2 mm thick.

Once you have reached the required thickness, pass the dough through the pasta machine a second time on the same setting – this helps to prevent the pasta from shrinking as you cut it.

Fit the appropriate cutter to the machine and pass the pasta through to cut your desired shape – tagliatelle, fettuccine, spaghetti or what you will.

If you are making shaped pasta, such as cappelletti (page 89), you should use the sheets of dough as soon as you have rolled them.

Alternatively you can, of course, roll and shape pasta the old-fashioned way, using a rolling pin and cutting it with a knife.

serving suggestions

• Toss plain pasta with seared cherry tomatoes flavoured with thyme flowers, and flakes of drained, canned tuna in olive oil.
• Try serving warm baby vegetables cooked à la grecque (see page 51) with olive pasta.
• Slices of grilled, very spicy sausage added to red pepper salsa (page 22) complement the flavour of my green olive pasta perfectly.

fettuccine with smoked mussels and pesto

You can smoke the mussels for this elegant pasta dish several hours in advance. Simply keep them in the fridge, covered with cling film so that they don't dry out. Steam for a few minutes just before serving. These quantities are appropriate for a starter, light lunch or supper. Increase the quantities to serve as a substantial main course. (Illustrated on page 46.)

Serves 4

1 kg lightly smoked Bouchot or Shetland mussels (page 47)
400g fettuccine, freshly made from 1 quantity pasta dough (page 84), or bought fresh pasta
4 tablespoons olive oil
juice of 1 lemon
1/2 quantity pesto (page 25)
salt and freshly ground pepper
4 basil sprigs, preferably purple, to garnish

Shell most of the mussels, keeping a few in their half-shell for garnish.

Bring a saucepan of salted water to the boil. Add the fettuccine with 2 tablespoons olive oil and cook for 3–4 minutes, until *al dente*. Drain and return to the pan. Add the remaining olive oil and the lemon juice. Season with pepper to taste, add the shelled mussels and toss lightly.

Immediately divide the fettuccine and mussels between 4 deep plates or shallow bowls. Arrange the reserved mussels on top, add a generous drizzle of pesto and put a basil sprig on the edge of each bowl.

wild mushroom cappelletti with herb salsa

I think of cappelletti as little cushions of happiness. I could eat them forever and they fully justify the time they take to make. Instead of a mixture of mushrooms, you could use just one flavourful variety, like ceps or morels.

When artichokes are in season, I include some cooked, finely diced artichoke hearts for a pleasant, nutty taste. In winter, I fill cappelletti with finely puréed Jerusalem artichokes or pumpkin purée flavoured with curry spices and a few finely snipped coriander leaves. Use these "little peaked hats" as a vehicle of discovery and let your imagination run riot …

Serves 6

500g pasta dough (page 84)

Filling:

600g wild mushrooms (girolles, chanterelles, ceps, horns of plenty etc, in equal amounts)
60g clarified butter (page 188)
60g shallots, peeled and chopped
40g flat-leaf parsley, chopped
salt and freshly ground pepper

To assemble and serve:

2 egg yolks, mixed with 2 tablespoons milk (eggwash)
flour, to dust
2 tablespoons groundnut oil
1 quantity herb salsa (page 24)
12 flat-leaf parsley sprigs, to garnish

To make the filling, cut off the base of the mushroom stalks and any earthy, gritty or damaged parts, using a small, sharp knife. Halve the horns of plenty down the middle and make sure they are free of debris or sand. If necessary, delicately and very briefly wash the different mushroom varieties separately in cold water and drain, or simply wipe them gently with a damp cloth. Chop the different varieties, keeping them separate.

Heat the clarified butter in a frying pan over a medium heat and put in the girolles and chanterelles. When they have exuded their liquid, add the horns of plenty and finally the ceps. Sauté briskly until all the liquid has evaporated. Add the shallots and cook for another minute. Scatter on the chopped parsley and season with salt and pepper. Set aside, while you roll out and cut the pasta.

Divide the pasta dough in half; keep one portion tightly wrapped. Roll the other half through the pasta machine into a long sheet, 2mm thick and about 11cm wide. Delicately brush off any excess flour. Using a large cook's knife, trim the edges to ensure a consistent width of 11cm, then cut into nine 11cm squares. Fill and shape to make cappelletti (see right), then place on a lightly floured tea-towel. Repeat with the rest of the pasta to make 18 cappelletti in total.

To cook the cappelletti, bring a pan of lightly salted water to the boil to which you have added the groundnut oil. Gently put in the cappelletti, reduce the heat to simmering point and cook for 5–6 minutes, until *al dente*.

To serve, lift the cappelletti out of the water with a slotted spoon, drain and place three on each warmed plate. Spoon a little herb salsa over each cappelletti, garnish with parsley sprigs and serve at once.

SHAPING CAPPELLETTI

Brush two adjacent sides of each square very lightly with eggwash.

Put a tablespoon (about 20g) of filling towards that corner, but stop just short of the line of the eggwash.

Fold the opposite corner on to the eggwashed corner to make a triangle, and press very lightly to seal the edges.

Trim the edges to neaten, then cut off the two points which form the base of the triangle.

Dab a little eggwash on to one of the cut ends and, stretching them gently, fold them up and over until the two points meet. Slide your index finger between the base of the cappelletti and the two sides, pressing them firmly between your thumb and index finger to seal them tightly.

guinea fowl and lamb couscous

I was introduced to couscous by Chougui, an Algerian cook, whose couscous was second to none. I like to use guinea fowl rather than the more traditional chicken. Sometimes I make it with pheasants, which are inexpensive and tasty, cooking the breasts for no more than 20 minutes, to keep them moist. The best accompaniment to this great winter dish is a glass of ice-cold water.

Serves 6

600g carrots, peeled and sliced into thick rounds
12 baby turnips, peeled
400g pumpkin, peeled, deseeded and cut into 6 chunks
400g courgettes, cut into almond shapes
1/2 white cabbage, halved
60g dried chickpeas, soaked in cold water for 24 hours and drained
100g currants, soaked in hot water for 30 minutes and drained
1 guinea fowl, about 1.5kg
1 shoulder of lamb, about 2kg, boned and trimmed of all fat and sinews
150ml groundnut oil
300g onions, peeled and cut into chunks
500g tomatoes, peeled, deseeded and cut into chunks
2 teaspoons sweet paprika
1 large bouquet garni, including 2 celery sticks
salt and freshly ground pepper

Couscous:

300g medium coarse couscous
300ml warm water

To serve:

10g coriander sprigs
50g pumpkin seeds, toasted
3 tablespoons harissa paste

Tie the carrots, turnips, pumpkin and courgettes in separate pieces of muslin, securing with long lengths of string. (This will prevent them from being crushed during cooking.) Tie each piece of cabbage in muslin and blanch in boiling water for 2 minutes.

Drain the chickpeas, put them in a saucepan, cover with cold water and bring to the boil. Immediately lower the heat and simmer gently for 2 hours. Drain, rinse in cold water, drain well and add to the currants.

Cut the guinea fowl into 6 pieces and the lamb into 3cm cubes; season both with salt. Heat 2 tablespoons oil in a large frying pan and fry the guinea fowl pieces to an appetising golden brown. Transfer to a plate and keep covered. Heat another 2 tablespoons oil in the pan, sear the lamb and fry until browned; transfer to a flameproof casserole or large saucepan.

Pour off the fat from the frying pan, add another 2 tablespoons oil and brown the onions gently. Add to the lamb. Put the tomatoes and paprika in the frying pan and cook gently for 5 minutes. Add to the casserole, then pour in cold water to cover generously. Bring to the boil over a high heat. Skim the surface and lower the heat to a bare simmer. Add the bouquet garni, cover and cook for 1 hour, skimming as necessary.

Add the guinea fowl thighs and legs, carrots and cabbage; cook for a further 55 minutes. Now add the guinea fowl breast pieces, the turnips, courgettes and pumpkin and cook for another 20 minutes.

Put the couscous in a bowl. Sprinkle on the warm water, whilst stirring the couscous with your fingertips. Leave it to absorb the water for 4–5 minutes. Moisten with 4 tablespoons oil, stirring with your fingertips to aerate the couscous, and salt lightly. Add the chickpeas and currants and transfer to the top of a steamer.

Put 2 large ladlefuls of the cooking liquor from the meat into the base of the steamer and steam the couscous over a medium heat for 30 minutes, stirring it with a fork every 10 minutes to ensure the grains cook evenly and don't stick together.

To serve, combine the meat and vegetables in a warmed bowl, pour over the cooking liquor and scatter with coriander. Pile the couscous into another warmed dish and sprinkle with pumpkin seeds. Dilute the harissa in 2 or 3 tablespoonfuls cooking liquor and serve it separately in a bowl to allow guests to spice up their couscous as they wish.

tabbouleh

Here is an innovative way to serve this popular Middle Eastern dish, which I adore making, especially when I am in Provence. Like risotto, there are countless versions; my favourite is intensely lemony and full of fresh parsley and mint. It tastes even better the day after it is made.

Serves 6

300g medium or coarse bulghur wheat
225ml cold water
300g very firm, ripe tomatoes
300g cucumber
6 small spring onions, including tender green leaves finely snipped
40g curly parsley, chopped
20g mint leaves, snipped
100ml olive oil
juice of 3 lemons
12 black olives, pitted and sliced
salt and freshly ground pepper

Garnish:

1 green pepper
6 inner Savoy cabbage leaves
2 limes, cut into wedges, plus 6 lime segments
6 mint sprigs, plus a handful of shredded mint
6 flat-leaf parsley sprigs
4 tablespoons chopped curly parsley

Put the bulghur wheat in a saucepan, add the water and bring to the boil over a medium heat, stirring occasionally. Cook for 10 minutes, then tip into a sieve, refresh under cold water for 30 seconds to stop the cooking and leave to drain thoroughly for 30 minutes.

Meanwhile deseed and finely dice the tomatoes. Peel and finely dice the cucumber. Sprinkle with salt, leave for 5 minutes, then drain and pat dry.

Tip the bulghur wheat on to a tea-towel, roll it in the towel to dry thoroughly, then place in a salad bowl. Add all the other ingredients and mix gently, seasoning to taste. Cover with cling film and leave in a cool place for at least 2 hours to let the flavours to develop.

To serve, peel the green pepper with a swivel peeler, then pare long, fine slices with the peeler. Line individual dishes with the cabbage leaves. Divide the tabbouleh between them, heaping it into a dome and arranging a few of the olive slices on the surface. Garnish each serving with green pepper strips, a lime segment and a little shredded mint.

Provide each guest with a dish containing a lime wedge, mint and parsley sprigs, and some chopped parsley, so they can flavour their tabbouleh to taste.

rice pilaff

I serve this pilaff as an accompaniment to my lobster fricassée with peppers (page 144), flavouring it with curry spices, a few toasted pine nuts and blanched sultanas. Flavoured with herbs rather than spices, it is delicious with steamed fish, such as my fillets of sea bass in green jackets (page 99). To serve the pilaff as a tasty starter, I add some sautéed chicken livers and sliced button mushrooms at the last moment.

Serves 4

60g butter
60g onion, peeled and finely chopped
200g long-grain rice
400ml boiling water
1 thyme or rosemary sprig, or 1 tablespoon ground curry spices (cumin, coriander, turmeric etc)
salt and freshly ground pepper

Preheat the oven to 200°C/gas mark 6. Melt the butter in a flameproof casserole, add the onion and sweat it gently for 1 minute. Add the rice, increase the heat very slightly and cook for about 2 minutes, stirring with a wooden spoon, until the rice becomes translucent.

Pour on the boiling water, add your chosen herb or spices and season sparingly with salt. Cover and cook in the oven for 18 minutes.

Leave the pilaff to rest, still covered, in a warm place for 8–10 minutes. Discard the herb, fork through the rice, season to taste and serve.

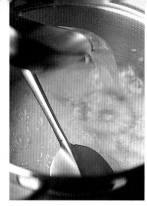

seafood risotto with crustacean essence

The correct way to make a risotto is a subject of debate amongst Italians – should you or should you not stir the rice as it cooks; must you use a wooden spoon? My only concern is to make a good risotto and this method works for me. Here marigolds give the rice a pale golden tint, which complements the prawns and cuttlefish perfectly, but they are not essential.

Serves 6

Risotto:

850ml fish stock (page 16)
100g butter
60g onions, peeled and finely chopped
200g risotto rice, preferably carnaroli
100ml dry white wine
2 edible marigolds (optional)
40g parmesan, freshly grated
salt and freshly ground pepper

Seafood, and crustacean essence:

18 large raw prawns in shell, cleaned
200ml cold fish stock (page 16)
24 cuttlefish or baby squid, preferably fresh, cleaned
2 tablespoons olive oil
10g butter

First make the risotto. Bring the fish stock to the boil in a saucepan and keep it at a simmer.

Melt 60g butter in a small saucepan, add the onions and sweat gently for 2 minutes, then add the rice and stir with a spoon. Increase the heat slightly

and continue stirring until the rice turns opaque and begins to "sing".

Pour in the wine, stir once only, then leave to cook until two-thirds of the liquid has evaporated.

Add two-thirds of the hot fish stock and a little salt. Stir once only and leave to cook gently for about 12 minutes, adding a little more hot stock if necessary.

Check the texture of the rice; it should be very firm, almost crunchy. Add the rest of the stock and cook for another 2–3 minutes.

Take the pan off the heat, add the marigold petals if using, sprinkle in the parmesan and stir in the remaining butter. Cover the pan with a lid and leave to stand off the heat for 6–8 minutes.

Put the prawns in a saucepan, cover with the cold fish stock and bring to the boil. Immediately take the pan off the heat and add the cuttlefish. Cover the pan and leave to stand for 3 minutes.

Drain the seafood, reserving the stock; keep the cuttlefish warm. Shell the prawns, reserving the heads, and add to the cuttlefish.

To prepare the crustacean essence, crush the prawn heads with the flat of a large knife. Place them in a small saucepan with the olive oil and colour over a high heat for 3 or 4 minutes. Add the reserved fish stock and whizz in a food processor for 3 minutes. Strain through a fine chinois or muslin-lined sieve set over a small saucepan. Reduce the resulting liquid to a slightly syrupy consistency. Remove from the heat and whisk in the butter.

Mix two-thirds of the prawns and cuttlefish into the rice. Divide between deep serving plates and arrange the rest of the seafood on top. Drizzle with a few drops of the reduction to serve.

steamed and poached dishes

Over the past decade, steaming has become one of my favourite cooking methods. It is extremely quick, and preserves the vitamins, colours and flavours of the ingredients better than any other form of cooking. It is ideal for preparing a light, healthy, digestible meal. You can either use a steamer or saucepan with a Chinese-style wooden steaming insert, flavouring the water in the pan with herbs and wine, or spices; or use a light stock. Apply salt directly to the food, rather than add it to the liquid.

One of my favourite dishes is my steamed poussins scented with ginger and lemon grass (page 100). These take very little time to cook, and I find the perfumed flavours of this utterly simple dish extremely seductive. Steamed rice makes the perfect accompaniment.

Green vegetables, especially asparagus, taste better and retain their qualities perfectly when they are steamed. My little steamed stuffed cabbages (page 99) can be prepared in advance, and need only 8 minutes cooking at the last moment. I even use steam to peel tomatoes and peaches; it takes only a few seconds and even preserves the flavour and colour of very ripe fruit.

Poaching is a delicate method of cooking. The temperature of the poaching liquid (water, court bouillon, wine, milk, sugar syrup etc) must always be kept at between 65° and 80°C. It is essential to obey this rule so as not to destroy the proteins of the ingredient you are poaching, so use a cooking thermometer.

Steaming makes fish more succulent and preserves their texture and intrinsic flavours. It is more suitable for pieces or fillets than whole fish. I often wrap the pieces in spinach or other leaves to protect them from the heat and seal in the flavours, as in my steamed fillets of sea bass in green jackets (page 99), for example. The only minus point is that, unlike poaching, you can not use the liquid as the base for a sauce.

I like to add dulse seaweed to the steamer for a couple of minutes just before serving steamed fish. I love its tender texture, mild flavour and attractive red colouring, which are all preserved by the last minute cooking. When steaming a 500g lobster, I embed it in a nest of seaweed so that during the 10 minutes or so it takes to cook, it absorbs the iodine flavour of the seaweed. It needs no other accompaniment than a vegetable *nage* (page 17).

Fish are equally good poached whole or in pieces. A whole poached trout *au bleu* occasionally appears as a speciality on my menu at The Waterside Inn. For my turbot poached in red wine (page 101), I use steaks; the outer part of the flesh is tinted by the red wine, while the centre remains white and firm-textured.

Most fruits are suitable for poaching. Vary the poaching liquid according to the texture of the fruit, using sugar syrup, sweet wine or water, and adding an appropriate herb or spice; rosemary, lavender mint, or cloves, for example. Or, for something out of the ordinary, you could use a flavoured tea, as I do in my poached apricots in assam tea syrup (page 111).

steamed fillets of sea bass in green jackets

This lovely, light dish is ideal for entertaining when time is short, since both the sauce and the fish can be prepared in advance. Simply reheat the coulis in a bain-marie and steam the sea bass 10 minutes before serving. You can use spinach leaves to wrap the fish, but lettuce has a more delicate texture and flavour, which complements the sea bass better. Rice pilaff flavoured with herbs (page 93), and cauliflower purée are unusual and delicious accompaniments.

Serves 4
4 portions of sea bass, about 180g each (cut from a good thick fillet from a 2.5kg fish)
8 attractive dark green outer lettuce leaves
salt and freshly ground pepper

To serve:
30g clarified butter (page 188)
deep-fried, shredded white part of 2 leeks
leek coulis with saffron and dill (page 27)

Remove the skin and season the fish with salt and pepper. Blanch the lettuce leaves and refresh, then drain. Wrap each sea bass portion in 2 lettuce leaves, then wrap each parcel in cling film.

Half-fill a steamer with water, and salt lightly. Bring to the boil, then lower the heat so that the water barely trembles. Put in the steaming rack, arrange the sea bass parcels inside, cover and steam for 8–10 minutes. To test whether the fish is done, insert a trussing needle or fine knife tip into the centre for 10 seconds; it should penetrate easily and feel hot when you remove it and place it on your inner arm.

To serve, carefully peel off the cling film from the fish parcels. Place one on each plate and brush with clarified butter. Make a little airy pile of deep-fried leek on top of each parcel and pour the leek coulis around the edge. Serve at once.

little steamed stuffed cabbages

Serve these cabbages as they are, brushed lightly with melted butter, or with leek coulis with saffron and dill (page 27). They go well with my roast stuffed Christmas goose (page 129). Prepare ahead if you like and chill until ready to steam.

Serves 6
2 potatoes (preferably Desirée), 300g total weight
200g clarified butter (page 188)
1 thyme sprig
1 head of broccoli, cut into florets and blanched
12 small Brussels sprouts, trimmed
1 medium Savoy cabbage, outer leaves removed
salt and freshly ground pepper

Peel the potatoes and cut into 1cm dice. Rinse and dry in a cloth. Heat the clarified butter in a saucepan over a medium heat, add the potatoes with the thyme and cook until just tender. Drain and put in a bowl with the broccoli. Season to taste.

Cook the Brussels sprouts in boiling salted water until tender. Refresh, drain and season. Put in a bowl.

Take off the cabbage leaves and blanch in boiling salted water for a few minutes. Refresh, drain and cut out the thickest part of the ribs if necessary.

To assemble the cabbages, place a double thickness of cling film, about 16cm square, on the work surface. Lay a cabbage leaf on it, season, and place a generous tablespoon of potato and broccoli mixture in the middle, then add 2 Brussels sprouts.

Fold the cabbage leaf over the stuffing to enclose it. Bring the 4 corners of the cling film together over the cabbage, turn over to enclose the cabbage ball tightly and knot the excess cling film to preserve the cabbage shape. Make 5 more "cabbages" in this way.

Fill a steamer pan with water, salt lightly, cover and bring to the boil. Put the stuffed cabbages in the top of the steamer, cover and steam for 8 minutes.

Lift out on to a plate, cut the cling film knots and gently invert the cabbages on to a serving platter, peeling off the cling film. Serve immediately.

steamed poussins scented with ginger and lemon grass

On a recent visit to Thailand, one of my former chefs, Marco Avitabilé (who now oversees the kitchens at the Grand Hyatt in Hong Kong) prepared a delicious chicken for me along the lines of this recipe. I have used poussin rather than chicken, and added a few variations of my own. The bouillon adds a peasant touch, which I adore. This dish should be eaten piping hot.

Serves 4

1.5 litres water
20g fresh root ginger, peeled and thinly sliced
2 lemon grass stalks, cut lengthways into thick julienne
2 poussins, each 350–400g, wishbones removed
250g broccoli florets
1 tablespoon cornflour, mixed with 2 tablespoons cold water
2 tablespoons groundnut oil
oil for deep-frying
100g rocket leaves
salt and freshly ground pepper

To serve:

200g fragrant Thai long-grain rice, freshly steamed

Put the water into the steamer pan, salt very lightly, cover and bring to the boil. Meanwhile, mix the ginger with the lemon grass and place inside the poussins; they don't need trussing. Put them in the top of the steamer, cover and steam for 15–20 minutes.

Scatter over the broccoli florets, and cook for another 2 minutes. Transfer the broccoli to a bowl, cover with cling film and keep warm. Cut off the legs and breasts from the poussins; wrap the breasts in foil and leave to rest in a warm place. Reserve the legs.

Break up the carcasses and put them in the cooking water in the base of the steamer, together with the ginger and lemon grass mixture (from inside the poussins). Simmer for 5 minutes, add the blended cornflour and cook, stirring, for 1 minute, then strain through a fine chinois into a saucepan. Adjust the seasoning if necessary; keep the sauce warm.

Heat the groundnut oil in a frying pan. Add the poussin legs, skin-side down, and fry over a medium heat until the skin is slightly crunchy and a beautiful light golden brown.

Heat the oil for deep-frying in a suitable pan to about 160°C. Make sure the rocket is completely dry. Put it into the hot oil and deep-fry until very crisp, as you would parsley, stirring with a slotted spoon. Lift out of the oil with the slotted spoon and drain on kitchen paper. If the rocket isn't as crisp as it should be, reheat the oil and fry it for another 2–3 minutes. Drain on kitchen paper and salt lightly.

To serve, pile the hot rice into a dome on a serving platter and arrange the poussin breasts and legs on top. Scatter on little heaps of broccoli and rocket, and serve the sauce separately.

turbot poached in red wine

Turbot, the "king of fish" is always best cooked on the bone, with its skin. My friend André Charial makes this powerful red wine sauce with Château de Romanin at the famous Ostau de Beaumanière. Its deep red colour contrasts superbly with the whiteness of the turbot, and it enhances the depth of flavour. If turbot seems too expensive, brill is an excellent alternative.

Serves 4
*4 turbot steaks on the bone, with skin, about
300g each (cut from half a 1.5kg turbot)
16 small new potatoes
$^1/_2$ lemon
1 bottle red wine (eg Côtes du Rhône)
75ml fish stock (page 16)
60g butter
salt and freshly ground pepper*

Sauce:
*250ml Château de Romanin, or Côtes du Rhône
20g shallot, peeled and finely sliced
20g button mushrooms, finely sliced
200ml veal stock, chicken stock (page 16) or
vegetable stock (page 17)*

Garnish:
4 deep-fried, tender sage sprigs

Season the turbot steaks lightly with salt and pepper; set aside.

Using a small sharp knife, pare the potatoes into mushroom shapes: make a 5mm horizontal cut around the circumference, about one-third down the length of each potato, to form the mushroom cap, then cut away the excess potato to shape the stalk (see photograph, above right). Put the potato "mushrooms" in a pan of lightly salted water, add the lemon (to prevent the potato disintegrating) and cook until tender. Leave the potatoes in the cooking water.

To make the sauce, pour the Château de Romanin into a small saucepan, add the shallot and mushrooms and reduce by two-thirds over a low heat. Add the stock and reduce again until the sauce lightly coats the back of a spoon. Pass the sauce through a fine chinois, season with salt and pepper and keep warm.

To poach the fish, put the turbot steaks, Côtes du Rhône and fish stock in a wide shallow saucepan and set over a medium heat. As soon as the liquid begins to bubble, reduce the heat to a bare simmer, no more than 80°C, and skim off any scum from the surface. Poach the fish for 15 minutes. To test whether it is cooked, insert a trussing needle or fine knife tip into the flesh for 10 seconds; it should penetrate easily and feel hot when you take it out. Lift out the turbot steaks and carefully remove the dark and white skin with a knife tip.

To serve, melt the butter, drain the potato mushrooms and roll them in the butter. Divide the potatoes between the plates. Place a turbot steak on each plate with a fried sage sprig to one side. Spoon a little sauce over the turbot and serve the rest of the sauce in a sauceboat.

OPENING OYSTERS

Hold the oyster in the palm of one hand, using a cloth for protection. Hold an oyster knife in the other hand and push the tip of the blade into the pointed end of the oyster.

Slide the blade all along the inner edge of the top shell so as to sever the muscle that joins the two shells.

Lift off the top shell, leaving the oyster in the lower shell.

Carefully release the oyster from the cupped shell and slide it into a bowl with its juices. Make sure you pick out any loose bits of shell. Rinse the cupped shells in cold water and reserve for serving the oysters.

poached oysters with mayonnaise and horseradish

Oysters poached like this are full of flavour, which is further accentuated by the mustardy mayonnaise and grated horseradish. Fresh-tasting watercress makes this dish easy on the palate. If you prefer, you can use flat native oysters, but I find them too rich and fatty. As with all shellfish, it is essential to use only the freshest oysters and to eat them within an hour of preparing the dish.

Serves 4

24 medium (size 2) rock oysters, opened
50ml dry white wine
500g watercress
250g mustardy mayonnaise (page 20)
2 tablespoons grated horseradish, preferably fresh
about 72 tiny tarragon sprigs
salt and freshly ground pepper
coarse sea salt, to serve

Tip the oysters and their juices into a saucepan, pour in the white wine and set over a medium heat. As soon as the liquid comes up to a gentle simmer, no more than 80°C, turn off the heat. The oysters will be poached in about 15 seconds. Keep them in their juices at room temperature.

Pick the leaves off the watercress, shred them and mix with 100g mayonnaise. Season to taste.

To serve, divide the watercress mayonnaise between the cupped oyster shells. Drain the oysters and place them on a tea-towel to dry for a few seconds. Put an oyster in each shell and season with half a turn of the pepper mill.

Coat the oysters with a little mayonnaise, leaving a border of watercress showing. Scatter a little grated horseradish over each oyster and lay 3 tarragon sprigs on top. Serve on a bed of coarse sea salt; this not only looks good, but holds the oysters steady.

poached cherries with creamy rice pudding

I often poach cherries in Banyuls, a strong, sweet red wine from the Roussillon region, which is served as an aperitif. I love to serve these poached cherries on rice pudding, scattered with very fine shreds of tender vanilla pods.

Serves 6

Rice pudding:
130g pudding rice
500ml milk
50g caster sugar
pinch of salt
1 vanilla pod, split lengthways, seeds scraped out
10g butter for greasing
1 egg yolk
60ml double cream

Poached cherries:
36 cherries
75g butter
75g caster sugar
400ml Banyuls
freshly grated nutmeg

To serve (optional):
2 or 3 soft-textured vanilla pods, finely shredded lengthways

First make the rice pudding. Rinse the rice in cold water, then put into a saucepan, cover with cold water and bring to the boil. In a large saucepan, heat the milk with the sugar. Drain the rice and add it to the milk, with the salt, and the vanilla pod and seeds. Cook for 10 minutes over a very low heat, then cover with buttered greaseproof paper so that the rice doesn't dry out, and cook for another 5 minutes.

Mix the egg yolk with the cream. As soon as the rice is cooked, remove from the heat and stir in the cream mixture. Remove the vanilla pod and cover the rice pudding again with the paper. Set aside at room temperature to allow the flavour to develop until ready to serve.

To prepare the cherries, remove the stalks and stone the fruit using a cherry stoner.

As you stone them, put the cherries into a bowl of iced water, to encourage them to plump up.

When you are ready to cook the cherries, drain them thoroughly. Heat a frying pan (preferably non-stick). When it is hot, put in the butter and heat until foaming. Quickly sprinkle in half of the sugar and add the cherries. Toss them 2 or 3 times, adding the rest of the sugar as you go, and cook for about 2 minutes.

Pour in two-thirds of the Banyuls. Flambé the cherries and shake the pan. Once the flames have died down allow the cherries to poach for a minute or two (depending on their ripeness), then transfer them with a slotted spoon to a deep plate.

Pour the remaining Banyuls into the pan and cook to a light syrupy consistency. Spoon this syrup over the cherries and stir in a pinch of nutmeg. For the best flavour, serve the cherries while they are still just warm, arranged around the warm rice pudding. Scatter the shredded vanilla pods if using, in the middle.

PEELING AND STONING PEACHES

Make an incision all round the circumference of the peach with the tip of a small knife.

Using a slotted spoon, carefully drop the peach into a saucepan of boiling water (see note).

As soon as the skin splits open at the point of incision, lift out the peach with the slotted spoon and put it into a bowl of water with ice cubes added.

Take out the peach and peel off the skin, using your fingertips or the tip of the knife; it will come away very easily. If you are not using the peach immediately, rub the flesh lightly with lemon juice to prevent discoloration.

To remove the stone, using a small knife and following the natural line, cut the peach in half through to the stone. Hold the fruit in the palm of your hand and twist the halves in opposite directions so that one comes away from the stone. Pull out the stone from the other half.

NOTE If the peaches are very ripe, steam them for a few seconds, rather than immerse them in boiling water to loosen the skins.

poached white peaches with pistachio crème anglaise

I have chosen to poach the peaches in their skins for this recipe, so that the beautiful colour of the skin tints the flesh. A judicious hint of rosemary added to the poaching liquid will develop and enhance the flavour of the fruit, but it is essential not to overdo it, or the delicate peach taste will be lost. (Illustrated on page 33.)

Serves 6
6 very ripe white peaches
150g caster sugar
a small branch of rosemary
500ml pistachio crème anglaise (page 32)
6 tiny mint sprigs

Put the peaches in a saucepan large enough to hold them in a single layer. Barely cover them with cold water and add the sugar and rosemary. Bring to the boil over a high heat, then immediately lower the heat and cook at a low simmer, about 90°C, taking care not to let the liquid boil. Poach the peaches for 5–10 minutes, depending on how ripe they are.

When the peaches are cooked, transfer them to a bowl with the poaching syrup and keep at room temperature until ready to serve. Like all poached fruits, they will taste better if they are not refrigerated.

Just before serving, lift the peaches out of the poaching liquid and peel them, with your fingers or a small knife. Halve the fruit and remove the stone.

Put two peach halves in each deep plate, pour a little pistachio crème anglaise around them, lay a sprig of mint on one side and serve at once.

rhubarb poached in citrus juice topped with coconut flakes

This light, refreshing dessert is so inviting that it will soon disappear...

Serves 4

500g rhubarb
juice of 4 oranges
juice of 1 lemon
250g caster sugar
1 fresh coconut

Peel the rhubarb stalks to remove the fibrous threads, then into 5–6cm chunks. Rinse in cold water.

Combine the orange juice, lemon juice and sugar in a saucepan. Bring to the boil over a low heat, stirring occasionally. Put in the rhubarb and poach for 3–5 minutes, depending on the thickness of the stalks and the ripeness of the fruit. Whatever you do, don't cook it for too long, or it will break down into fibres.

Using a slotted spoon, carefully transfer the rhubarb to a bowl, then reduce the cooking juice by half. Strain it through a fine chinois on to the rhubarb. Leave to cool, then refrigerate for about 1 hour.

To open the coconut, hold it in a cloth in one hand above a bowl (to catch the liquid, which makes a refreshing drink) and, using your other hand, bang it with a hammer or rolling pin.

To serve, divide the rhubarb and juice between serving bowls or small deep plates. Hold the coconut directly above the bowls and scrape the side of a spoon across the flesh, so that curls of different shapes and sizes fall on to the fruit. Serve at once.

poached pears in sauternes

These soft, refreshing winter fruits, with their complex texture and flavour, make the perfect finish to a meal. It is best to serve the pears cold, but absolutely not chilled. Any excess syrup can be churned to make an excellent pear sorbet.

Serves 6

6–12 ripe pears, depending on size (preferably William or Conference)
juice and pared zest of 1 orange
375ml Sauternes, or other not-too-sweet white wine
750ml water
50g honey
200g sugar
juice of 2 lemons
1 vanilla pod, split
1 cinnamon stick, broken into short lengths
4 cloves

Using a small, sharp knife, score a zigzag pattern in the skin around the top of each pear, working downwards from the stalk. Leaving the zigzag skin at the top in place, peel the rest of each pear very thinly so as to preserve their shape (see photograph). Remove the core from the base, using a corer or small melon baller. Cut the orange zest into thin strips.

Combine all the ingredients in a saucepan big enough to hold everything, including the pears. Set over a medium heat until the liquid comes to the boil, then reduce the heat so that it is barely simmering. The cooking time will vary according to the ripeness of the pears. Very ripe pears will only take 5 minutes; much less ripe fruit will need up to 15 minutes. As soon as they are ready, turn off the heat.

Transfer the pears with their poaching syrup to a bowl and leave at room temperature until needed.

Serve one or two pears on each plate with a little orange zest and some of the syrup.

lightly jellied red fruit consommés

These glorious jellies inspire romance. To enjoy them at their best, use very ripe, flavourful fruit at the height of the season, and serve as a dessert or pre-dessert.

Serves 8

200g strawberries
200g raspberries
200g redcurrants
200g cherries
3 star anise, or the pared zest of 1 orange, whichever you prefer
100g caster sugar
150ml cold water
4 gelatine leaves, softened in cold water
juice of 1 lemon
redcurrant sprigs, wild strawberries, lavender sprigs or gooseberries, to decorate

Wash each type of fruit separately, then hull the strawberries and raspberries if necessary; strip the redcurrants off their stalks with the prongs of a fork; stone and halve the cherries. If the strawberries are large, halve them too.

Put all the fruits in a saucepan with the star anise or orange zest, sugar and water. Cover the pan tightly with cling film and stand it in a bain-marie. Poach over a low heat at 70–80°C for about 40 minutes.

Thoroughly drain the gelatine. Take the saucepan out of the bain-marie, uncover and gently stir in the gelatine to dissolve it. Cover with fresh cling film and leave to cool at room temperature.

Strain the fruit through a muslin-lined sieve or fine chinois into a bowl. Add the lemon juice to the liquid. Pour this consommé into small glasses and refrigerate for several hours until lightly set.

Take out of the fridge about 20 minutes before serving and keep at room temperature. Decorate each glass with a sprig of redcurrants, wild strawberries, sprigs of lavender or a gooseberry.

poached apricots in assam tea syrup

These poached fruits are delicious served on their own in some of their tea-flavoured syrup, or with sugar-glazed slices of brioche (illustrated on page 187). You only need to allow three apricots per serving, as they swell slightly during cooking.

Serves 8

24 moist dried apricots
250g caster sugar
500ml water
2 tablespoons Assam tea leaves

Put the apricots in a bowl. Combine the sugar and water in a saucepan and dissolve over a medium heat. Bring to the boil, then pour over the fruit and leave at room temperature for 12 hours.

Pour the syrup into a saucepan; cover the apricots and set aside. Heat the syrup to 70°C (barely simmering), take the pan off the heat and add the tea. Cover and leave until almost cold.

Strain the cooled syrup through a fine chinois on to the apricots. Leave to infuse for at least 12 hours, to allow the apricots to absorb the aroma of the tea.

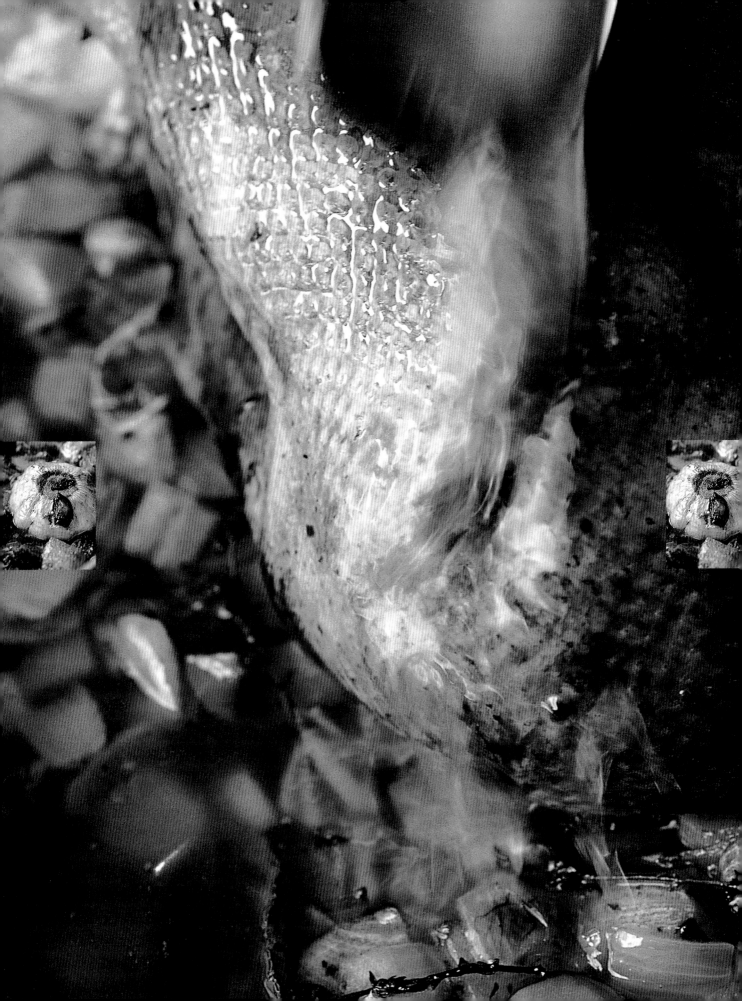

grills, roasts and bakes

Grilling has become increasingly fashionable because it's one of the healthiest cooking methods. I use a ridged griddle pan, which must be preheated until very hot to sear the food on the outside and give an attractive lattice marking, but not overheated or the food will acquire a bitter taste. In the same way, a barbecue must be very hot before food is put on the grid. After 5–10 minutes cooking, I reduce the heat under the griddle pan, or move food to the sides of the barbecue, so that heat penetrates the centre of the food evenly and gently.

Take meat out of the fridge an hour or two before roasting, and preheat the oven to very high for at least 20 minutes, then adjust the setting according to the recipe. Brush the meat with melted butter or oil to help it brown evenly, and baste frequently with the cooking juices or fat to keep the flesh succulent. Halfway through cooking, turn the meat, taking care not to pierce it or the juices will run out. Wrap the cooked meat in foil and leave to rest for about 10 minutes, so that the flesh relaxes and the juices are retained as you carve it.

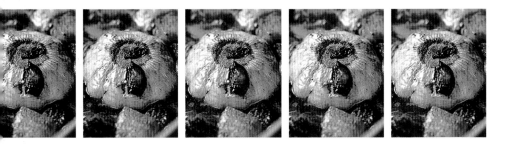

As for poultry and game birds, I always remove the wishbone before cooking; this makes carving easier and you can cut the breast into nice even slices. I often bard the birds with thin slices of back fat to make them more tender and succulent.

Small pieces of meat and poultry, and brochettes are delicious grilled, and fill the kitchen with appetising aromas. Seafood and crustaceans are equally divine; serve these the moment they are cooked.

When barbecuing, I like to add vine shoots to the charcoal to impart a subtle, succulent flavour. Once the grid has cooled a little, I barbecue asparagus, slices of aubergines and courgettes, or tomato halves, brushed with olive oil. I serve these drizzled with a trickle of olive oil, a few drops of balsamic vinegar and snipped basil … and enjoy the explosion of flavours in my mouth.

Roasting, which exposes every side of the food to the heat, is more suitable for larger pieces of meat or fish. The traditional Sunday roast, an occasion when the whole family gathers at the table, may be a custom that is fast disappearing, but it's one that we should protect: "the family that eats together stays together".

Always use a roasting pan large enough to allow you to surround the roast with aromatic vegetables like carrots, onions, celery and garlic; these will flavour the jus. Tender roast vegetables (page 124) make a fresh, colourful dish, which I top with a slice of goat's cheese.

For baked dishes en croûte, like my châteaubriand in a brioche crust (page 138), and sea bream in a fine salt crust (page 134), it is essential to turn the tray during cooking to ensure a superb, evenly golden crust and uniform cooking throughout.

I also use the oven to dry very thin slices of garlic, courgette, beetroot, mushrooms and fennel; fruits like apple and pineapple, and citrus zest. These are scattered on a baking sheet lined with baking parchment and dried at 60–80°C for an hour or two, depending on thickness and water content. I use a few of these attractive "crisps" to garnish roast meat, poultry or fish, and my salade gourmande.

chicken breasts with fennel

This utterly simple dish is full of flavour. For an equally good low-fat version, replace the butter and fennel seeds with the candied zest of a lemon.

Serves 4
4 boneless chicken breasts
2 fennel bulbs
2 large carrots, peeled
2 tablespoons olive oil
40g butter
2 tablespoons fresh fennel seeds
salt and freshly ground pepper

Marinade:
2 tablespoons runny honey
juice of $^1/_2$ lemon
4 tablespoons olive oil
pinch of cayenne pepper

Mix all the marinade ingredients in a wide, shallow bowl, adding a little salt. Add the chicken breasts and turn them to coat thoroughly. Cover with cling film and leave for 1 hour, turning them halfway through.

Cut the fennel lengthways into 5mm thick slices. Blanch in boiling water for 5 minutes, refresh and drain. Cut the carrots into 5mm diagonal slices. Score the surface, then blanch for 3 minutes; refresh and drain. Lightly brush the fennel and carrots with oil.

Heat a griddle pan until smoking hot. Add the fennel and griddle for 2 minutes, then add the carrots and griddle for a further 3 minutes, giving them a quarter-turn to mark a lattice. Turn over and repeat on the other side. Season, place on a plate and keep hot.

Put the chicken pieces in the hot griddle pan, skin-side down. Once they are marked with lines, quarter-turn to make a lattice pattern. Turn them over, lower the heat and give them a quarter-turn as before. Cook for 12–15 minutes in total, depending on thickness.

Arrange the fennel slices on plates and top with the chicken. Place the carrots alongside. Put a knob of butter on each chicken breast and top with fennel seeds.

medallions of roe deer with green peppercorn butter

Roe deer venison is a delicate meat that should be treated simply, to preserve all its savours. Fillets of chamois and red deer can be cooked in the same way. I love to serve this dish with green olive pasta (page 84).

Serves 4
1 fine fillet of roe deer venison, 600–800g
salt and freshly ground pepper
watercress leaves, to garnish

Marinade:
100ml olive oil
few thyme sprigs
2 bay leaves, quartered
2 garlic cloves, peeled and thinly sliced
10 black peppercorns, crushed
5 juniper berries, crushed

Green peppercorn butter:
100g butter, softened
juice of 1 lemon
16 green peppercorns in brine, rinsed and crushed

Cut the venison fillet into 8 medallions. Mix together all the marinade ingredients. Put the medallions into a deep dish, cover with the marinade (for method, see quick meat marinade, page 14), and leave to marinate for 1 hour.

Meanwhile, mix together the ingredients for the green peppercorn butter and season with a little salt.

Heat a griddle pan until very hot. Season the medallions very lightly, put them on the griddle and cook for 1 minute, then give them a quarter-turn to obtain a lattice marking. Cook for another minute, then turn them over and repeat. The precise timing will depend on how well done you like your meat.

To serve, place 2 medallions on each plate and top with a generous amount of the flavoured butter. Garnish with a few watercress leaves on the side.

grilled fillet of lamb with mediterranean vegetables

This is one of the recipes I love to cook when I stay at my house in the south of France. The confit vegetables add an unusual modern twist, and the dish brings together many of the typical products of the region.

You will need to debone a whole saddle of lamb (or get your butcher to do this for you); keep the bones to make the jus. Much of the dish can be prepared in advance, as you can cook the vegetables beforehand and keep them covered. Just reheat them and the jus a few minutes before you assemble the dish. Only the meat needs to be cooked at the last moment.

Serves 4

2 lamb fillets from a saddle, trimmed of all fat and
membrane, each about 220g (bones reserved)
1 onion, peeled and cut into small pieces
1 carrot, peeled and coarsely chopped
100ml dry white wine
6 savory sprigs
1 small bouquet garni
200ml water
1 courgette, about 200g
2 aubergines, preferably long thin ones, about 350g
in total
75ml olive oil
300g confit tomatoes (page 79)
4 unpeeled confit garlic cloves (page 80), optional
8 black olives, stoned and cut into small strips
salt and freshly ground pepper

First make the jus: Preheat the oven to 220°C/gas mark 7. Put the lamb bones in a roasting pan and place in the hot oven to colour for 15 minutes. Add the onion and carrot, cook until browned, then deglaze the roasting pan with the white wine and simmer until reduced by half. Transfer everything to a saucepan and add 2 savory sprigs, the bouquet garni and water. Cook gently until reduced by half, then strain through a muslin-lined sieve. Pour the jus back into the saucepan, return to the heat and reduce to a slightly syrupy consistency. Season with salt and pepper and keep at room temperature.

To grill the vegetables, heat a ridged griddle pan. Using a mandoline or sharp knife, cut the courgette and aubergines into long slices, about 3mm thick. Lay these flat on the work surface, season with salt and brush with a smear of olive oil. Place in the griddle pan and grill for 30 seconds – 1 minute, depending on the heat of the pan, until marked with brown lines. Give the vegetables a quarter-turn to make a criss-cross pattern, then turn them over and repeat on the other side. Put all the grilled vegetables on a plate and keep them warm.

To cook the lamb fillets, smear both sides and the cut ends with a touch of olive oil and grill in the same way as the vegetables until marked with an attractive lattice pattern on both sides; they will now be cooked pink. If you prefer lamb cooked further, roast them in a hot oven for 5 minutes for medium, or 10 minutes for well done. Wrap the fillets loosely in foil and leave to rest for 5 minutes before carving.

To assemble the dish, unwrap the lamb, season with salt and carve into thin slices. Lay a slice of aubergine on each plate. Place a few warm confit tomatoes on top, cover with a courgette slice, add a few more tomatoes, then another aubergine slice. Finally add half a sliced lamb fillet to each serving. Top with a confit garlic clove if using. Pour the warm jus over the meat and vegetables, scatter on a few olive strips, lay a sprig of savory in the jus on one side of each plate and serve straight away.

fish brochettes

Spices give these unusual brochettes a special flavour – mustard intensifies the taste of the monkfish, while cumin seeds give the salmon a sweet spiciness. Lime leaves protect the scallops from the heat and impart a subtle flavour. The potatoes hold the fish in place, and taste good too. You will need 20cm skewers; if wooden, pre-soak in warm water to prevent burning. Salad leaves are the ideal accompaniment; or you might like to serve a hollandaise sauce (page 20) spiked with a spoonful of fresh tomato coulis.

Serves 4

220g middle-cut salmon fillet, skinned
180g monkfish fillet, from the middle or head end
1 teaspoon cumin seeds
1 tablespoon English mustard powder
4 shelled plump scallops, each about 60g
4 fresh lime or lemon leaves, blanched (optional)
2 tablespoons olive oil
4 small new potatoes, par-boiled and halved widthways
salt and freshly ground pepper

To serve:

rocket, purslane or mâche (lamb's lettuce)
fennel fronds (optional)
lemon wedges

Cut both the salmon and monkfish fillet into 4 cubes. Roll the salmon in cumin seeds. Carefully dry the monkfish cubes, then roll in the mustard powder. Lightly salt the scallops. Smear the lime leaves with olive oil, then roll one around each scallop.

Thread a potato half on to each skewer, with the rounded side facing outwards. Add a monkfish cube, then a wrapped scallop, a piece of salmon and finally another potato half.

Preheat the grill or barbecue until very hot. Drizzle a trickle of olive oil over the brochettes, salt them lightly and grill for 4–5 minutes, turning every minute; the fish will be lightly cooked. If you prefer, cook it for a further 2–3 minutes.

Place a brochette on each plate and arrange a few salad leaves to one side, scattering with some fennel fronds if you like. Serve with lemon wedges.

grilled lobster with garden herbs

A garnish of asparagus tips will set off this simple, delicate dish to perfection. For an extra treat, serve with a hollandaise sauce (page 20).

Serves 4

4 live lobsters, each about 400g
8 tablespoons olive oil
juice of 1 lemon
few rosemary sprigs, 2 thyme sprigs, 1 dill sprig and 2 tarragon sprigs
small bunch of flat-leaf parsley
salt and freshly ground pepper
small bunch of watercress, to garnish
1 lemon, cut into wedges, to serve

Put the lobsters in a plastic bag in the freezer for 2 hours, then remove from the bag and plunge into a large pan of boiling water for 30 seconds. Drain and split them in half lengthways with a large knife, starting at the head and pressing down firmly, then repeating at the tail end. Remove the gritty sac from the head, the intestines and black intestinal thread. Reserve the coral if any, to use in a sauce.

For the marinade, mix 4 tablespoons olive oil with the lemon juice in a dish and put in the lobster halves, flesh-side down. Leave to marinate for 20 minutes.

Meanwhile, chop all the herbs very finely and mix with the remaining 4 tablespoons olive oil.

To cook, preheat a griddle pan. When it's very hot, season the lobsters with salt and place, flesh-side down, on the griddle. Cook for 2 minutes, giving them a quarter-turn to obtain a lattice marking, then turn them over and cook for another 2–3 minutes; to check that they are tender, pierce with the point of a knife.

Place 2 lobster halves on each plate, flesh-side up. Season with pepper and drizzle with a few drops of herb oil. Garnish with watercress and serve with lemon.

quail brochettes with almond-stuffed dates

The world has been my inspiration for these extraordinary brochettes – China for the spice and mushrooms, the Middle East for dates and nuts, and Italy for the mozzarella.

They are ideal for a summer barbecue. In winter, you can cook them in a griddle pan. When fresh almonds are out of season, use dried ones and soak them in cold water for at least 24 hours.

For an extra touch of exoticism, I serve the brochettes on a bed of dark rice, using two-thirds wild rice and one-third black rice. The black rice gives a softer texture to the wild rice, which is rather too spiky on its own.

Serves 4
4 plump quails
8 fresh dates
8 skinned almonds, preferably fresh (or blanched)

Marinade:
1 tablespoon honey
1 tablespoon lemon juice
1/2 teaspoon five-spice powder

Skewers:
2 large onions, preferably red
handful of coarse salt
8 dried Chinese wood ear mushrooms, soaked in cold water for 6 hours
1 red pepper, halved, cored and deseeded
8 mini mozzarella balls
2 tablespoons olive oil
salt and freshly ground pepper

Preheat the oven to 200°C/gas mark 6. Put the marinade ingredients in a small saucepan, stand it in a bain-marie and bring to the boil, stirring occasionally, then set aside to cool.

Part-roast the onions in their skins on a bed of coarse salt for 20 minutes and leave to cool. Drain the soaked dried mushrooms and cook in lightly salted water for 20 minutes, then drain and set aside.

Meanwhile, stone the dates and insert an almond into the cavity.

To prepare the stuffed quail, remove the wishbone, using the point of a small knife.

Using a boning knife, carefully cut the meat from the breastbone, following the contours of the bones, and making sure the 2 breast fillets are held together as one piece. (Keep the legs to use in another dish, or grill them and serve to accompany the brochettes.)

Lay the butterflied quail breasts skin-side down and make an incision in the thickest part of each fillet.

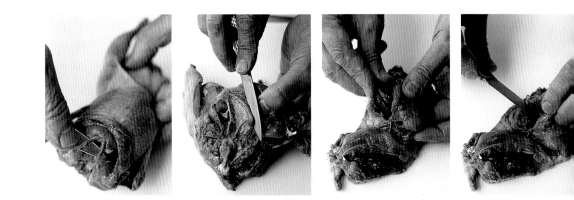

Insert a date in each incision in the quail fillets. Add the stuffed quail breasts to the cold marinade and leave for about 30 minutes, turning them over after 15 minutes.

Close the butterflied quail breasts, and secure the opening with cocktail sticks.

It is best to use metal skewers for the brochettes. Cut the red pepper into eight 3 cm squares. Skin and quarter the part-roasted onions, then thread a quarter on to each skewer. Wrap each mini mozzarella in a Chinese mushroom and thread one on to each skewer, followed by a red pepper square. Carefully thread a stuffed double quail breast on to each skewer. Next, thread on a square of pepper, another mushroom-wrapped mozzarella ball and finally another onion quarter. Brush the brochettes with a touch of olive oil and salt them lightly.

If possible, cook the brochettes on a barbecue, or use a hot griddle pan. Turn them every 2 minutes, allowing 8 minutes if you like your quail cooked pink, or 10 minutes if you prefer them medium. Slide the contents of the skewers delicately on to a bed of boiled dark rice. If you like, cut the quail fillets in half to reveal the almond-stuffed dates.

grilled confit of rabbit and apples with walnuts

This dish takes very little time to put together. The fruity flavour of the grilled apples marries very well with the rabbit, while the radicchio and mâche salad adds a refreshing note. (Illustrated on page 81.)

Serves 4
4 confit rabbit legs (page 80)
4 confit rabbit shoulders (page 80)
2 small apples, preferably Cox or Reinette
3 tablespoons walnut oil
1 tablespoon cider vinegar
200g radicchio or treviso, separated into leaves and washed
100g mâche (lamb's lettuce) in bunches, washed
8 walnuts, preferably "wet", peeled, halved and soaked in a little milk
salt and freshly ground pepper

Set a large griddle pan over a high heat. Put in the rabbit legs and cook for 2–3 minutes, then give them a quarter-turn to make an attractive criss-cross pattern. After another 2–3 minutes, turn them over and repeat on the other side. Reduce the heat and move the rabbit legs to the edge of the griddle, where it is less hot. Put the shoulders in the middle of the pan and cook in the same way as the legs. After 8–12 minutes, all 8 pieces will be ready. Remove them from the griddle and keep warm.

Cut the apples horizontally into rings, about 5 mm thick. Place them on the very hot griddle and grill for about 1 minute on each side, giving them a quarter-turn halfway through.

To assemble the dish, make a vinaigrette with the walnut oil, cider vinegar and a little salt and pepper. Use it to dress the radicchio and mâche salad. Arrange a bouquet of salad on 4 serving plates and prop a rabbit leg and shoulder against the salad. Put 2 apple rings on one side of each plate. Drain the walnut halves and divide them between the plates.

tender roast vegetables with goat's cheese

This refreshing starter, with its myriad of colours, flavours and textures, is a feast for the eye as well as the palate. Depending on the season and what's in the market, you can substitute any delicate vegetables, as long as they are tender.

Serves 4

12 small, young artichokes (the kind you can eat whole), optional
50ml dry white wine
100ml olive oil
juice of $1/2$ lemon
1 red and 1 green pepper
1 small aubergine
4 baby courgettes
1 small fennel bulb, peeled
8 baby corn cobs
12 asparagus tips
4 unpeeled garlic cloves
2 medium red onions, peeled and cut into wedges
2 thyme sprigs
2 bay leaves
18 seedless black grapes, peeled and halved
30g caster sugar
12 cherry tomatoes
50g pumpkin seeds
4 slices of creamy goat's cheese, cut from a log
salt and freshly ground pepper

If you are including artichokes, cut off the tips of the leaves, using a sharp knife, and pare the base to leave only the tender part of the stalk and the heart. Put the artichokes in a small saucepan with the white wine, 1 tablespoon olive oil and the lemon juice. Add sufficient water to cover and cook gently for 4 minutes, until half-cooked and still slightly crunchy. Leave the artichokes in their cooking liquid at room temperature until cold, then drain them.

Preheat the oven to 200°C/gas mark 6. Peel the peppers with a swivel peeler, halve them lengthways, remove the seeds and white membranes and cut the peppers into thin strips. Cut the aubergine and courgettes into 1cm thick rounds.

Par-cook the fennel in boiling water for 8 minutes, refresh, drain and cut into 8 wedges. Cut each baby corn cob into 3 pieces, blanch in boiling water for 3 minutes, refresh and drain. Blanch the asparagus for 2 minutes, then refresh and drain.

Heat 3 tablespoons olive oil in a small roasting pan, add the garlic and onion segments and brown them lightly for 2–3 minutes. Add the thyme and bay leaves and place in the oven.

Heat 2 tablespoons olive oil in a frying pan. Season the aubergine rounds with salt and pepper and fry over a medium heat on both sides until golden. Remove and set aside at room temperature.

Heat another 3 tablespoons oil in the pan. Add the pepper strips, sweat and colour them for 5 minutes, then add them to the onions (in the oven).

Add another 6 tablespoons olive oil to the frying pan, put in the courgettes, fennel and artichokes, and fry over a medium heat for 3 minutes. Add the baby corn and fry for another 2 minutes. Transfer the contents of the frying pan to the roasting pan and return it to the oven.

In a small frying pan, sauté the grapes with the sugar over a high heat until lightly caramelised, then add them, the aubergines and the asparagus, to the other vegetables in the roasting pan.

Heat the remaining olive oil in the same frying pan, add the tomatoes and cook over a medium heat until golden. As soon as they are coloured, put them with all the other vegetables. Using a slotted spoon, delicately stir all the vegetables together and season to taste. Roast in the oven for a further 5 minutes.

Lightly salt the pumpkin seeds, sprinkle with a few drops of olive oil and toast lightly under a low grill. Divide the vegetables between 4 plates, piling them into a dome. Remove the thyme and bay leaves. Scatter over the toasted pumpkin seeds, top with a slice of goat's cheese and serve piping hot.

roast leg of lamb with garlic and fresh anchovies

Before roasting a leg of lamb, I like to remove the bone and stud the meat with garlic and fresh anchovy fillets, a combination that imparts a superb flavour. The roasting time will, of course, be determined by the weight, and whether you like your lamb rare, medium or well done.

Lamb on the bone can be roasted in the same way, though it takes less time to cook because the bone conducts the heat through the meat. Simply omit the anchovies, stud the surface with the halved garlic cloves and allow 10 minutes per 500g after the initial roasting.

Serves 8

1 leg of lamb, about 2.5kg
8 fresh anchovy fillets, frozen until firm
3–4 garlic cloves, peeled and halved
50g softened butter, or clarified butter (see page 188)
2 carrots, peeled and roughly chopped
2 medium onions, peeled and quartered
1 head of garlic (unpeeled), halved widthways
2 bay leaves
few thyme or rosemary sprigs
salt and freshly ground pepper

Jus:

200ml red or white wine, according to taste
300ml water

Preheat the oven to 220°C/gas mark 7. Tunnel into the meat using a boning knife: working from the ball end, cut around the exposed bone, working deeper and cutting through the tendons to free the bone. Cut out the cartilage, then remove the bone from the other end. Reserve the bones and trimmings.

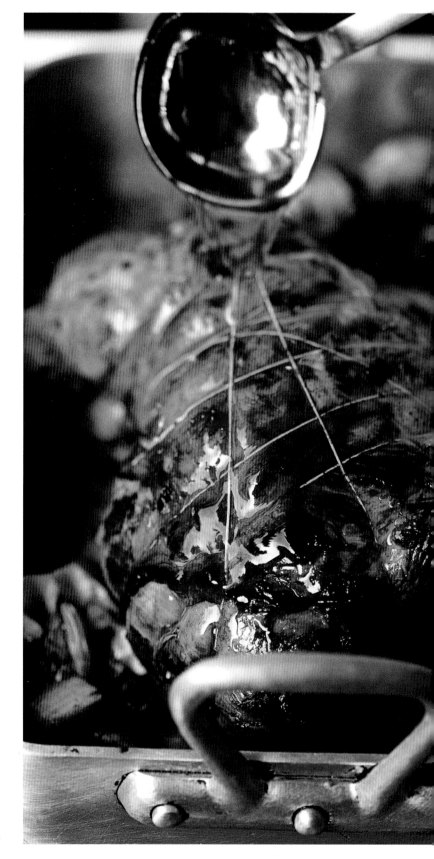

Make 6–8 incisions in the lamb with the tip of a pointed knife, spacing them well apart. Insert a frozen anchovy fillet in each cut and push it right into the meat, using the knife tip. Do the same with the 3–4 halved, peeled garlic cloves, making a small incision for each and pushing them in.

Tie up the lamb with string, securing it in about a dozen places to make a neat roast. Rub the surface with softened or clarified butter and season with salt. Put the lamb in a medium roasting pan. Scatter the carrots, onions, halved garlic bulb and herbs around the meat, then finally, add the bones and trimmings.

Roast in the oven for 50 minutes initially. Baste the lamb with the cooking juices and return it to the oven. Roast for a further 12 minutes per 500g for pink lamb, basting the meat every 15 minutes or so, and turning it over on to the other side halfway through to ensure even cooking and prevent the meat from

drying out. (If you prefer your lamb cooked for longer, allow 16 minutes per 500g for medium, or 22 minutes per 500g for well done lamb.)

To check if the lamb is cooked, insert a fine skewer into the thickest part of the meat for 10 seconds. Take it out and press it against your wrist; if it feels warm, the lamb is cooked. The juices that run from where you pierced the meat should be almost clear and transparent.

Take the lamb out of the roasting pan and wrap it loosely in foil; leaving a gap for air to enter will prevent further cooking and stop the meat from steaming. Leave to rest for 15–20 minutes before carving; this allows the meat to relax and helps to keep in the juices, making the meat beautifully tender. Meanwhile, make the jus (see below).

Once the meat has rested, carve it into even slices. Arrange on plates and spoon over some of the jus. Serve accompanied by vegetables of your choice, with the remaining jus handed separately in a sauceboat.

Jus

To make the jus, tip the pan and ladle out most of the fat that runs into the corner.

Set the roasting pan over a medium heat. Pour in the wine to deglaze the pan, lightly scraping the base of the pan to dissolve the sediment that has stuck to it.

Cook until the wine has reduced by half, then add 300ml water. Reduce the liquid again by half. Strain it though a fine sieve or muslin to obtain a light gravy or jus. Season to taste with salt and pepper. It is important to add the pepper at the end of cooking to ensure all of its pungency is retained.

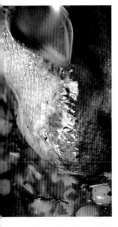

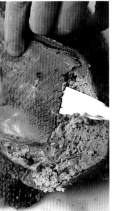

roast stuffed christmas goose

This superb Christmas or New Year dish makes a change from the traditional turkey, which appears too often for my taste on such occasions. Little steamed stuffed cabbages (page 99) are the perfect accompaniment. Any leftover goose and stuffing makes a delicious cold feast, served with my pickled damsons (page 188).

Don't try to use a food processor to mince meat for a stuffing; if you do not have a mincer, ask the butcher to mince the pork and fat for you.

Serves 8

1 goose, about 4kg, with a little of the neck skin attached
200g onions, peeled and cut into large pieces
200g carrots, peeled and cut into large pieces
small bunch of thyme
2 bay leaves
200ml dry white wine
200ml water
salt and freshly ground pepper

Stuffing:

800g pork back fat
400g streaky bacon
40g curly parsley, chopped
100g onion, peeled and chopped
40g butter
200g button mushrooms, chopped
2–3 teaspoons salt
³/₄ teaspoon freshly milled pepper
100g crustless white bread, diced and soaked in 200ml milk
2 eggs
200ml double cream, well chilled
50ml Cognac (optional)

First make the stuffing. Put the pork and bacon through a mincer, using the medium grille. Place in a bowl with the parsley. Lightly sweat the onion in the butter until softened, then add the mushrooms and cook until

tender. Add to the meat with the seasoning. Stand the bowl over another bowl of crushed ice and work the mixture with a wooden spoon for 3–4 minutes, until well mixed. Lightly squeeze the bread to remove excess milk, then add to the mixture, with the eggs. Mix for 2 minutes, then add the cream, and Cognac if using, and work the mixture for another 3–4 minutes. Cover with cling film and refrigerate until needed.

Preheat the oven to 180°C/gas mark 4. Lift up the skin covering the front of the goose breast and take out the wishbone with a small knife. Turn the goose over on to the breast, and season the body cavity with a generous pinch of salt. Stretch out the neck skin as far as it will go, and put on as much stuffing as you can, pushing it as far towards the start of the breast as possible. Fold the skin back over the stuffing and using a trussing needle threaded with kitchen string, sew up the skin to make a sort of jabot, so that the stuffing cannot escape during cooking. Put the goose into a roasting pan (without added fat, as it's a fatty bird). Place any remaining stuffing on a lightly buttered sheet of foil, and roll up into a fat sausage shape.

Roast the goose in the hot oven for 30 minutes. Baste with the fat that is rendered, then pour off most of it, and add the onions, carrots, thyme and bay leaves to the pan. Roast for a further 1¹/₄ hours, basting every 20 minutes. Put the stuffing "sausage" (if you have made one) into the roasting pan alongside the goose after the first 20 minutes.

Transfer the cooked goose to a serving platter, cover loosely with foil so that the skin remains crisp and leave to rest in a warm place. Leave the stuffing in its foil roll, and set aside with the goose.

To make the jus, pour off the fat from the roasting pan. Set over a high heat and deglaze with the wine. Reduce by half, then add 200ml water, reduce by half again, and strain through a chinois. Season to taste, and keep warm. To serve, using scissor tips, carefully cut the string that is holding the stuffing in the neck skin, and discard it. Unwrap the stuffing "sausage" and cut it into slices.

Carve thin slices of breast meat. Cut off the legs from the carcass, serving only the thigh meat cut into long slices. Serve the goose with a little stuffing from the neck or "sausage", and the jus.

roast duckling with cloves, honey and spices

This springtime dish is very popular at The Waterside Inn. My manager, Diego Masciaga, carves it in the dining room with magical dexterity, into elegant thin slices, to the admiration of all my guests. Don't forget to warn your guests to pick out the cloves with their fork and discard them, as they have a very aggressive taste.

The perfect garnish for these ducklings with their oriental overtone would be pak choi tempura. Add an extra 2 teaspoons cornflour to the tempura batter (page 152), to make the deep-fried pak choi leaves extra crunchy.

Serves 4

2 Challandais or Gressingham ducklings, each about 1.4 kg, wishbones and feather ends removed, and trussed
20 cloves
100g runny honey
juice of $1/2$ lemon
1 tablespoon olive oil
generous pinch of pain d'épices spices (ground mixed ginger, cloves, cinnamon and star anise)
150g onions, peeled and cut into medium dice
150g carrots, peeled and cut into medium dice
2 thyme sprigs
300 ml chicken stock (page 16), or water
salt and freshly ground pepper

Preheat the oven to 200°C/gas mark 6. Bring a large saucepan of lightly salted water to the boil. Put in the ducklings and blanch them for 3 minutes. Transfer to a bowl of iced water and leave for 5 minutes, then drain well and pat dry.

Stick the cloves into the duckling breasts, spacing them evenly and well apart.

Mix the honey with the lemon juice, olive oil and ground spices. Put the ducklings in a roasting pan, brush generously with the honey and spice mixture, and immediately place in the hot oven. Roast for 5 minutes.

Baste the duckling with the liquid bubbling in the pan. Spread the onions, carrots and thyme around the ducklings, and continue to roast for another 20 minutes for pink duck, basting after 10 minutes. If you prefer your duck cooked medium to well done, roast for a further 10 minutes.

When the ducklings are cooked, cut off the legs, wrap the rest of the birds loosely in foil and keep them warm. Grill the legs for about 10 minutes, preferably in a griddle pan, giving them a quarter-turn after 2–3 minutes to give an attractive lattice marking, then turning them over to repeat on the other side.

To make the sauce, deglaze the roasting pan containing the honey-caramelised vegetables with the stock or water. Set over a medium heat, reduce the liquid by two-thirds to make a slightly syrupy sauce, then strain it through a chinois. Season with salt and pepper and keep warm.

To serve, carve off the duck breasts. Cut each twice on the diagonal, first in one direction, then in the other, to obtain 6 good chunky pieces from each breast. Arrange 6 pieces pell-mell on each plate, and place a leg on one side. Spoon off any grease from the sauce, then drizzle a few drops of sauce around the plates. Serve the rest separately in a sauceboat.

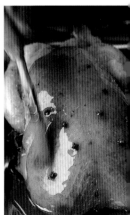

roast-poached stuffed loin of pork

This double cooking method of roasting and poaching makes the meat appetisingly golden on the outside, yet wonderfully succulent on the inside, and produces a rich, yet delicate gravy. I like to serve the pork with braised chicory and steamed or boiled mangetout; the contrasting melting and crisp textures are perfectly balanced.

Serves 4

750g boned loin of pork (about 1kg on the bone)
200g pig's caul, or 2 very thin strips of pork fat
60g clarified butter (see page 188)
2 carrots, peeled and chopped
1 onion, peeled and chopped
1.5 litres chicken stock (page 16)
1 bouquet garni
salt and freshly ground pepper

Stuffing:

20g butter
20g salt pork belly, finely diced
20g celery, finely diced
20g onion, peeled and finely chopped
40g apple, peeled, cored and chopped
60g Victoria or quetsche plums, stoned and finely diced
pinch of sugar
2 tablespoons coarse dried white breadcrumbs
2 tablespoons chopped parsley

First make the stuffing. Heat the butter in a saucepan, add the diced pork belly and cook until golden brown. Transfer to a bowl with a slotted spoon and reserve.

Add the celery and onion to the pork fat in the pan and sweat gently for 2 minutes. Add the apple, plums and sugar and cook over a medium heat for about 20 minutes, stirring with a wooden spatula from time to time.

Now add the breadcrumbs, parsley and fried pork, mix well and cook over a low heat for 5 minutes, stirring continuously. Season the stuffing to taste with salt and pepper. Transfer to a bowl and leave to cool, then cover and refrigerate for at least 2 hours.

To prepare the loin of pork, use a carving knife with a very long, thin, pointed blade to make an incision all the way through the middle of the meat. Using a circular sawing movement, cut out a small hole. Pull out the knife blade, making sure that all the meat from inside the hole comes out with it, leaving a cavity for the stuffing.

Insert a funnel with a fairly wide nozzle into one end of the cavity. Put in half the stuffing and push it in with your thumb. Repeat from the other end. Wrap the caul or pork fat around the pork loin to prevent the stuffing escaping from either end, and tie it in place with a few knots of kitchen string.

The first cooking stage is roasting the pork. Preheat the oven to 220°C/gas mark 7. Melt the clarified butter in a roasting pan. Put in the stuffed pork, season with salt and pepper and cook for about 6 minutes, until coloured all over. Add the carrots and onion and roast in the hot oven for 35 minutes, basting with the cooking juices every 10 minutes.

Now it is time to poach the pork. Pour the chicken stock into a long, shallow pan and bring to the boil. Put in the pork, carrots and onion, taking care not to include any of the cooking fat. Add the bouquet garni and poach at 70°C for 50 minutes, skimming off any scum from the surface whenever necessary. Lift out the pork and remove the string and caul or fat. Wrap the pork loin in foil and keep it warm.

Reduce the cooking liquor over a high heat until it very lightly coats the back of a spoon. Discard the bouquet garni. Season the gravy with salt and pepper to taste, then pass it through a chinois into a jug or bowl; keep hot.

To serve, carve 3 or 4 neat slices per serving. Arrange on plates, with the accompanying vegetables. Spoon the gravy over the pork, taking care to avoid drizzling any over the stuffing.

sea bream in a fine salt crust

My son Alain created this recipe, which he often cooks at The Waterside Inn. It reflects his talent for artistic simplicity, which I admire. Baking the sea bream in a salt crust highlights both the visual impact of the marbled flesh and the flavour. Other fish, such as sea bass, can be cooked in the same way.

Serves 2

1 sea bream, about 800g, gutted through the belly, gills removed, scaled and trimmed
3 thyme or fennel sprigs
3 herb crêpes (page 58), 26–30cm diameter

Salt crust:

80g egg whites
500g fine salt

Garnish:

50ml chive oil (page 188), optional
2 lemon wedges

Lay the fish on a double thickness of foil and put the thyme or fennel sprigs inside the belly. Trim the foil with scissors, following the contours of the fish and leaving a 2cm border all round; set aside.

Lay 2 crêpes on the work surface, overlapping them slightly, and place the sea bream on top (see above). Fold the crêpes over the fish to enclose it.

Use the third crêpe to cover the exposed parts, trimming it with scissors if necessary. The fish should be completely covered, but the crêpes must only overlap very slightly.

Preheat the oven to 200°C/gas mark 6. Sprinkle a little fine salt on to the centre of a baking sheet (this helps the fish to cook evenly). Lay the foil on the salt, then place the fish on the foil.

For the salt crust, beat the egg whites until half-risen, then add the salt and continue to beat until the whites are firm and smooth, like a meringue. Using a palette knife, spread evenly over the entire surface of the bream, taking it right down to the foil to make an airtight seal. Smooth the surface, then using the end of a small palette knife, trace the head, mouth and eye of the fish. Press down very lightly with the end of the palette knife to imitate scales (see below right) and finally trace the tail.

Very carefully transfer the baking sheet to the oven, taking care not to jolt it, which might cause the foil holding the fish to slip on the salt.

Bake for 20 minutes, then insert a trussing needle into the thickest part of the fish for 10 seconds to check if it is cooked; the needle should feel just hot when you withdraw it. If it is lukewarm, the fish needs a little longer.

Serve the bream without delay, presenting it in its salt crust to your guest. You can either leave it on the baking sheet, or slide it on the foil on to an oval platter lined with a napkin. At the table or in the kitchen, use a knife tip to cut open the crust, following the traced line of the head, then along the length of the body. Lift off the salt crust to release an instant waft of sea-scented steam, then carefully lift off the crêpes and peel away the skin with the knife blade to reveal the natural perfection of the fish.

Lift off the fillets with a knife and arrange them on 2 plates. If you wish, drizzle with chive oil, and garnish with lemon wedges. (Illustrated on page 6.)

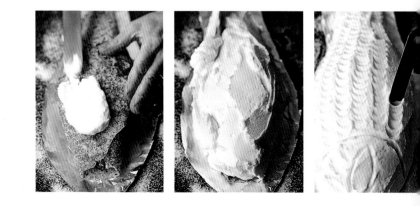

salmon en papillote with pine needles

I adore this dish, which Alain put together. As the salmon cooks, the pine needles infuse it with their flavour in an extraordinary way. The technique is simple, but the concept is brilliant. Serve with lemon wedges, and lettuce dressed with olive oil vinaigrette; or a light *nage* with star anise and a few pieces of sea lettuce added.

Serves 4

4 pieces of unskinned salmon fillet cut from the back, each about 220g
1 tablespoon white peppercorns, crushed
1 1/2 teaspoons coriander seeds, crushed
2 tablespoons Maldon salt flakes
100ml olive oil
120g long, marine pine needles, lightly rinsed in water if necessary and dried

Preheat the oven to 180°C/gas mark 4. Make two light incisions in the skin of each salmon fillet with a knife. Mix together the crushed pepper, coriander and salt flakes. Smear both sides of the fillets with olive oil and sprinkle the flesh side with the seasoning mixture. Roll the pine needles in the remaining olive oil.

Cut a double thickness of foil into four 25cm squares. Divide the pine needles into 4 portions. Put two-thirds of each portion in the centre of each foil square. Place a salmon fillet on top, skin-side down, and sprinkle with the remaining pine needles.

Loosely fold up the ends of the foil to meet in the middle, fold them over and pinch the edges together to seal, without wrapping the fish too tightly.

Place the papillotes on a baking tray. Put this on a heat diffuser or direct heat for 5 minutes, then transfer to the oven and cook for 5 minutes if you like your salmon pink in the middle. Give it another 5 minutes in the oven if you prefer it well done.

To serve, slide the papillotes on to serving plates, open them up to reveal the contents and present to your guests so they can appreciate the aroma. Remove the pine needles before the salmon is eaten.

minted carrot and pumpkin pastilla

New season's carrots and pumpkin infuse this flaky hors d'oeuvre with sweet, spicy nuances, while a squeeze of orange juice adds freshness.

Serves 6

600g pumpkin or squash, peeled and cubed
100ml olive oil
80g new or baby onions, peeled and thinly sliced
600g new carrots, cut into thin rounds
30g pine nuts, lightly toasted
50g sultanas, blanched in sugar syrup (page 188)
1 teaspoon grated fresh root ginger
large pinch of ground cinnamon
2 tablespoons snipped mint
12 sheets of filo pastry, trimmed to 21cm rounds
salt and freshly ground pepper
icing sugar, to dust
1 orange, cut into 6 wedges, to serve

Preheat the oven to 180°C/gas mark 4. Steam the pumpkin cubes until almost disintegrating, place in a bowl and crush with a fork. Heat a little oil in a saucepan, add the onions and sweat over low heat for 2 minutes. Add the carrots and cook gently to soften; they should retain a slight crunch. Add to the pumpkin with the pine nuts, sultanas, ginger and cinnamon. Mix well, season and stir in the mint. Cool completely.

Oil a deep ovenproof earthenware or cast-iron dish, 16cm in diameter. Lay a sheet of filo in the dish, brush with oil, then place another filo sheet on top and brush with oil. Spread a thin layer of the vegetable mixture on top. Continue to layer in this way to use all the filling and filo, finishing with two layers of oiled filo. Bake in the oven for 15–20 minutes.

Dust the cooked pastilla with a veil of icing sugar, and briefly place under a hot grill until the sugar is slightly melted; take care not to let the filo burn. Slide the pastilla out of the baking dish on to a serving plate, or serve it straight from the dish. It will crumble as you cut it, but this won't spoil the appearance. Serve with orange wedges.

châteaubriand
in a brioche crust

The difference between this recipe and a classic châteaubriand en croûte is the brioche crust, which is crisp and golden on the outside, yet meltingly soft inside. I serve it with a hollandaise sauce (page 20) enhanced with a generous handful of snipped chervil. The combination of mushrooms, beef and sauce is exceptionally good. When fresh ceps are in season, I use them instead of button mushrooms.

Normally a châteaubriand is a beef fillet cut to serve two, but this dish is better suited to serving four. It can be assembled up to 3 hours before the final cooking – ideal for entertaining.

Serves 4

*800–900g trimmed fillet of beef, cut from the top
end of the fillet down to the middle
60g clarified butter (page 188)
12 good spinach leaves*

Mushroom duxelle:

*40g butter
400g button mushrooms, wiped and finely chopped
juice of 1 lemon
60g shallots, peeled and finely chopped
60ml double cream*

To assemble:

*400g brioche dough (page 186)
flour for dusting
3 herb crêpes (page 58), 26–28cm diameter
1 egg yolk beaten with 1 teaspoon milk (eggwash)
salt and freshly ground pepper*

First make the mushroom duxelle. Heat the butter in a frying pan over a medium heat. Add the mushrooms and lemon juice and cook for a few minutes, until all the liquid has evaporated. Add the shallots and cook until softened, then add the cream and cook, stirring continuously, until it is all absorbed. Season to taste,

transfer to a bowl and leave to cool, then refrigerate.

To pre-cook the beef, preheat the oven to 200°C/gas mark 6. Heat the clarified butter in a roasting pan. Season the beef with salt and pepper, put it in the roasting pan and sear over a medium heat for 3–5 minutes, until golden brown all over. Put the pan in the oven and roast the beef for 7 minutes, turning it over halfway through. At this stage, the beef will be very rare. Take it out of the oven, place on a rack and leave to cool at room temperature.

Briefly blanch the spinach leaves, refresh and spread out to drain on a tea-towel.

To assemble, roll out the brioche dough on a lightly floured surface to a rectangle, roughly 25x35cm, 3mm thick. Lay 2 crêpes slightly overlapping along the middle, letting them overhang the ends by about 5cm. Cover with a few spinach leaves. Using a spoon, spread a 1cm band of mushroom duxelle down the middle of the crêpes. Put the cold fillet of beef on top and cover the whole surface, including the ends, with the remaining duxelle. Drape the rest of the spinach over the duxelle, then fold the crêpes up over the beef and cover it with the unused crêpe (halved if necessary). The beef should now be snugly wrapped.

Lightly brush the short ends of the brioche with eggwash. Fold one long side over the beef, brush with eggwash, then fold the other long side over the top. Roll out the brioche ends and trim to make 8cm flaps. Brush lightly with eggwash and fold them up over the fillet. Hold a baking sheet at a 45° angle against the side of the brioche-wrapped beef, then tilt and invert the parcel on to the baking sheet with the join underneath. Refrigerate for 30 minutes.

Preheat the oven to 220°C/gas mark 7. Brush the brioche crust with eggwash and use a knife tip to mark a lattice or leaf pattern. Cut a small vent in the middle to let the steam escape during cooking. Bake in the oven, allowing 25 minutes for rare beef, 35 minutes for medium and 45 minutes for well done. If the brioche crust starts to look too brown during cooking, cover it with baking parchment or foil.

Lift the châteaubriand on to a rack and leave to rest for 5 minutes, then cut into 1.5–2cm thick slices. Place on warm plates and serve at once.

pan-fries, sautés and deep-frying

I offer several pan-fried main course dishes on my restaurant menu. Pan-frying is ideal for cooking small, tender pieces of poultry, fish and meat, like tournedos, lamb chops and my pigeon canoes (page 146). These dishes are cooked *à la minute*, so my customers can order them cooked precisely to their liking, from *bleu* to well done.

For pan-frying, I use a straight-sided frying pan made from tinned copper or stainless steel with a heavy base, and a little clarified butter or hot (but not smoking) groundnut oil. I salt the food just before

cooking, but add pepper at the end so it retains its aroma. The food needs to be turned in the pan with tongs (rather than a fork) until it reaches a light golden colour; it is sometimes then necessary to partially cover the pan to finish cooking.

Sautéed dishes are cooked uncovered at a higher temperature, and should be fried to a dark nutty brown. Before serving sautéed and pan-fried food, leave it to rest briefly on a rack while you degrease the pan and deglaze it with a little wine, water or light stock to make a quick, light flavourful jus.

Veal medallions and chops have a tendency to become dry during cooking. To avoid this, first sear them on both sides in a little clarified butter, then throw this away, replace it with fresh butter and finish the cooking over a very low heat to keep the meat moist and succulent, especially if you like it pink.

Stir-frying in a wok is one of the fastest cooking methods, which I use to preserve the colours and firm texture of the ingredients, as in my lobster fricassée with peppers (page 144). As it comes into contact with the hot wok, the lobster flesh acquires a light golden crust on the outside, while remaining juicy and moist in the centre. A wok is the perfect utensil for cooking lobster, langoustine, squid and vegetables.

When deep-frying, you need to use very fresh oil heated to between 160°C and a maximum of 190°C, depending on what you are frying. A light haze rising from the oil indicates that it is too hot, which can be extremely dangerous, so I strongly recommend that you use a deep-frying thermometer to keep a check on the temperature.

The basic rules for deep-frying are:

• Never fry wet ingredients, or the oil will boil over.

• Fry ingredients in small batches, otherwise the temperature of the oil will drop and the food will absorb too much grease.

• Drain the fried food for a few seconds and place it on kitchen paper before serving.

• When making French fries, use two pans if possible. Heat the oil in one to 120–130°C, and the other to 176°C. Cook the French fries for 2–3 minutes at the lower temperature, then fry in the other pan until crisp and golden.

• Take great care when deep-frying to avoid accidents, and never let children anywhere near the pan.

When the deep-frying oil is cooling and is around 60°C, add a couple of lightly beaten egg whites; these filter the oil and catch any scraps of food. Strain the oil through a chinois to use another time.

pan-fried skate wings with cherry tomatoes

Blanching skate wings before pan-frying makes them more succulent, and I find the crispy, bones at the thin end of the wings utterly divine. Cherry tomatoes are a refreshing alternative to butter or a sauce, or even lemon. Serve with a side salad.

Serves 4

4 skate wings, each about 250g, skinned
500ml milk
2 thyme sprigs
2 bay leaves
50ml olive oil
1 garlic clove, peeled and thinly sliced
4 clusters of cherry tomatoes on the vine, soaked in cold water for 20 minutes
100g clarified butter (page 188)
80g butter
about 40 small capers, deep-fried for 1 minute
salt and freshly ground pepper

Put the skate wings in a shallow pan and cover with the milk; if necessary, add some cold water to ensure that they are completely immersed. Add the thyme and bay leaves, salt lightly, and set over a medium heat. When the liquid has bubbled a few times, take the pan off the heat. Leave the skate wings in the liquid for 3 minutes, then drain and wrap in a well-dampened tea-towel.

Preheat the oven to 100°C/gas mark 1/4. Mix the olive oil with the garlic. Drain the tomatoes and brush them generously with the garlicky olive oil. Sprinkle with a little salt, and arrange on a rack set over a baking tray. Cook in the oven for about 20 minutes.

To cook the skate, quickly heat the clarified butter in one or two frying pans. Thoroughly pat dry the skate wings with kitchen paper, season with salt, and cook in the very hot butter for 3 minutes. Turn them over with a palette knife and cook for another 3 minutes; during this time, lift up the skate wings slightly and pop a few knobs of butter underneath.

To serve, place a skate wing on each plate and sprinkle with fried capers. Arrange a cluster of tomatoes on one side of each wing. Serve at once.

pan-fried monkfish with red pepper confit

The success of this recipe depends on the cooking of the monkfish, which must be precisely timed. The thickness of the medallions will vary according to the size of the monkfish tail from which they have been cut, and this will determine the cooking time. The firm, yet succulent texture of the fish contrasts well with the melting confit peppers.

Serves 4

250g confit sweet red peppers (page 79)
4 medallions of monkfish, each about 160g
100ml olive oil
few rosemary sprigs
4 garlic cloves, peeled and thinly sliced
2 tablespoons snipped parsley
salt and freshly ground pepper
1 lemon, quartered, to serve

Warm the confit red peppers in their own oil.

Pat the monkfish dry with kitchen paper and season lightly with salt. Heat the olive oil in a frying pan over a high heat, add the monkfish medallions and cook for about 2 minutes on each side, depending on their thickness, until golden brown. Halfway through cooking, sprinkle the medallions with rosemary.

To serve, divide the confit peppers between the plates, and arrange a monkfish medallion across them. Add the garlic to the oil remaining in the pan and fry until golden and crisp. Scatter the garlic and parsley over the monkfish and season with pepper. Place a lemon quarter on each plate and serve at once.

lobster fricassée with peppers

This rapid cooking method ensures that the lobster retains all its flavour and wonderful texture. Eat it the moment it is cooked, before the flesh firms up. Serve with rice pilaff or, for a lighter accompaniment, a refreshing stir-fry of pak choi and carrot rounds.

PREPARING LIVE LOBSTER

Place the live lobster in a plastic bag in the freezer for 2 hours, then remove from the bag and plunge into a large saucepan of boiling water for 30 seconds.

Twist off the claws, then separate them from the elbow and crack them with the knife blade.

Use the knife tip to separate the head and body.

At the end of the body, just above the tail fin, make an incision with the knife tip on either side of the tail, leaving 2–3mm in the centre of the carapace intact. Hold down the tail fin with your fingers and twist and pull it to separate the body and extract the intestinal tract. Discard the tract. Using the knife, cut the lobster into 3 chunks, following the line of the articulations.

Cut off two-thirds of the antennae on the head. Split the top of the head shell diagonally for the presentation, lift it off and scrape out any grit from the inside with the knife tip.

Split the rest of the head, scrape out the coral, remove the membrane and discard the gritty stomach sac. Cut the edible parts of the head and the legs into pieces to use for the sauce. Put the claws, elbows, tail chunks and the head shell on a plate. Sprinkle with a mixture of salt and cayenne pepper just before cooking.

Serves 4

4 live lobsters, about 400g each
2 teaspoons salt
1 teaspoon cayenne pepper
60g clarified butter (page 188)
2 green peppers, cored, deseeded and thinly sliced
100ml port (preferably white)
24 coriander leaves
rice pilaff (page 93), to serve

Prepare the lobsters (see left). Mix the salt with the cayenne and sprinkle over the lobster pieces.

Heat half the clarified butter in a wok set over a very high heat. Put half the lobster pieces in the wok and cook over the high heat for about 3 minutes, stirring every 20–30 seconds, until they are coloured and cooked all over.

Scatter over half the peppers, pour on half the port and continue to cook for 30 seconds, still over a very high heat. Transfer the lobster pieces, except the claws, to a bowl. Cook the claws gently for another minute, then add to the bowl with the cooking juices. Cover with foil and keep warm. Cook the rest of the lobster in the same way.

Using poultry shears, cut off the membrane from under the shell on the lobster chunks. Put a mound of rice pilaff in each of 4 deep plates and place the presentation head shells on top. Arrange the lobster pieces all around and pour the cooking juices over the chunks. Scatter over the coriander and serve at once, with the rice pilaff.

pigeon canoes
with grape jus

This is an excellent way to serve pigeon or squab.
Pan-frying makes the flesh soft and tender, and
the taste is enhanced by the grape-flavoured jus.
Crisp cabbage and melting chestnuts provide
contrasts in texture. Most of the preparation can
be done in advance; simply pan-fry the pigeon at
the last moment.

Serves 4

4 oven-ready pigeons or squabs
200g clarified butter (page 188)
1 carrot, peeled and chopped
1 onion, peeled and chopped
400g white grapes
40g caster sugar
100ml dry white wine
1 bouquet garni
16 fresh chestnuts, or vacuum-packed
peeled chestnuts
300ml milk
1/2 medium Savoy cabbage, cored and
thinly shredded
salt and freshly ground pepper

To prepare the pigeons, cut off the legs with a knife
and bone the thighs. Lift up the skin covering the
front of the breasts and remove the wishbones. Keep
all the bones to make the jus. Using poultry shears, cut
the carcasses diagonally, starting below the wings and
under the breast fillets. Each pigeon will be in two
parts: the breasts on the bone with the wings attached
(the "canoe"); and the back of the carcass. Chop the
carcasses; remove any remaining giblets.

To make the jus, put 50g clarified butter in a
saucepan with the chopped carcasses, reserved leg
bones and wishbones (and the pigeon necks if you
have them). Brown over a medium heat, then lower
the heat, add the carrot and onion, and sweat gently
for 5 minutes. Tip the contents of the pan into a sieve
to get rid of the fat, then return them to the pan.

Set aside 24 of the best grapes for the garnish.
Add the rest to the pan, sprinkle with sugar and cook
gently for 5 minutes, stirring occasionally. Deglaze with
the wine, reduce it by half and add enough water to
barely cover the bones. Bring to the boil, immediately
lower the heat and skim the surface. Add the bouquet
garni and bubble gently for 45 minutes. Pass through
a muslin-lined chinois into a small pan and reduce the
jus to a slightly syrupy consistency. Cover and set aside.

If using fresh chestnuts, heat the grill to high.
Lightly pierce the rounded side of the chestnuts with a
small, sharp knife. Place them on a baking sheet and
put them under the hot grill until the shells blister and
start to split open. Remove and cover with a tea-towel.
One at a time, remove the shells and skins with a
small, sharp knife. Put the peeled chestnuts in a small
saucepan with the milk and cook very gently for about
20 minutes, until tender. Cover the pan and leave the
chestnuts to cool in the milk. Peel and deseed the
reserved grapes for the garnish.

Heat 75g clarified butter in a frying pan. Add the
shredded cabbage and cook over a high heat, stirring
frequently, until just cooked but still *al dente*. Season
with salt and pepper, take off the heat and keep the
cabbage warm.

To cook the pigeons, season them, and heat the
remaining clarified butter in a deep frying pan. Add
the canoes and cook over a medium heat for 6–8
minutes, turning them to colour all over. Add the legs
and cook in the same way for 8 minutes. The pigeons
will now be cooked pink. If you prefer them medium,
cook for another 5 minutes. Cover the pigeon with foil
and rest in the pan for a few minutes before serving.

To serve, drain the chestnuts and pour on a little
boiling water. Drain thoroughly, making sure you
eliminate any milky skin. Put the chestnuts and the
reserved grapes in the saucepan containing the jus.
Heat gently for about 5 minutes, until the jus just
starts to bubble; immediately remove from the heat.

Pile the cabbage in the middle of 4 plates. Put a
pigeon canoe on top of each mound, flanked by the
legs. Arrange the chestnuts and grapes around the
cabbage and sprinkle with a spoonful or two of jus.
Serve the remaining jus separately in a sauceboat.

stir-fried vegetables

Stir-frying or "wok-ing" is a very quick method of cooking, in which the colours and flavours of the ingredients remain natural and at their best. Stir-fries not only look and taste delicious, but they are light and healthy, too.

Serves 2

1 tablespoon clarified butter (page 188)
2 carrots, peeled and cut into rounds
4 small pak choi hearts
1 head of broccoli, cut into florets
12 mangetout
$^{1}/_{2}$ red pepper, cored, deseeded and cut into batons
6 baby corn cobs, halved lengthways
2 tablespoons vegetable stock or water
1 garlic clove, finely chopped; or 1 teaspoon grated fresh ginger
1 teaspoon sesame oil
salt
flat-leaf parsley or coriander sprigs, to garnish

Place the wok over a high heat until smoking, then add the clarified butter.

Add the vegetables to the wok, one variety at a time, starting with the carrots and pak choi. Cook for 30 seconds, stirring continuously with a spatula, or tossing them in the wok with a flick of the wrist. Next, add the broccoli, then the mangetout, still stirring or tossing. Add the red pepper and finally the baby corn.

Season with a little salt, add the vegetable stock or water and cook for 2–3 minutes, according to how crisp you like your vegetables. Add the garlic or ginger and stir-fry briefly. Quickly drizzle over the sesame oil.

Serve garnished with parsley or coriander sprigs.

special pan-fried rib of beef

This is more of a technique than a recipe. Red meat that is pan-fried or roasted conventionally always requires a resting time of 10–20 minutes, to allow the flesh to relax and the blood to disperse through it. However, this original method of cooking the meat en papillote before pan-frying allows you to serve it immediately, with delicious results. The same method can be applied to a châteaubriand.

I like to serve the beef accompanied with stir-fried vegetables (see left). When ceps are in season, I sometimes serve a cep coulis (page 25) as a treat.

Serves 4

1 rib of beef, about 800g trimmed weight, 5cm thick
80g clarified butter (page 188)
salt and freshly ground pepper

Brush the beef very lightly with clarified butter, then wrap it very tightly in a sheet of foil to make a well-sealed parcel.

Heat a dry frying pan until very hot. Put in the foil-wrapped beef and cook over a medium heat for 3 minutes. Turn it over without piercing the foil, and cook for another 3 minutes.

Remove the beef parcel from the pan, wipe the pan with kitchen paper, put in the remaining clarified butter and return it to the heat.

Unwrap the beef, salt it lightly, then put it back in the frying pan. Cook over a medium heat for 7 minutes on each side if you like it rare. If you prefer it medium to well done, cook it for a further 5 minutes on each side.

To serve, carve the meat on the diagonal as soon as it is cooked. Place two slices on each plate, grind over a twist of pepper and serve immediately.

vegetable tempura

I serve this tempura the moment it comes out of the oil, with curry mayonnaise for dipping.

Serves 6

about 24 French beans
12 cauliflower florets, cut into 5mm slices
12 broccoli florets, cut into 5mm slices
12 mushrooms, halved or quartered if large
12 baby courgettes with flowers, prepared
(see left)
sesame oil (preferably untoasted), or groundnut
oil for deep-frying

Tempura batter:

45g cornflour
185g plain flour
1/2 teaspoon bicarbonate of soda
1/2 teaspoon Maldon salt flakes
475ml ice-cold, lightly carbonated mineral water
(eg Badoit or San Pellegrino)

To serve:

curry mayonnaise (page 20)

PREPARING BABY COURGETTES WITH FLOWERS

Delicately open up the flower and cut out the stamen with a small sharp knife.

Use the knife to cut out the calyxes that lie at the base of the flower.

Cut the end of the courgette into a "V" to resemble an arrow tip. Starting at about 1.5cm from the base of the flower, make a series of incisions, cutting through the courgette at 2mm intervals all along its length, to make a kind of fan. The courgette is now ready for deep-frying.

Plunge the French beans into boiling water and immediately refresh in cold water; drain and pat dry.

To make the batter, put the dry ingredients into a bowl. Mix in the carbonated water a little at a time, stirring with long chopsticks; do not over-mix. Don't worry if the batter looks slightly grainy; this is quite normal. Use the batter straightaway.

Heat the oil in a wok or deep-fat fryer to 160–180°C. Cook the tempura a few at a time, coating each vegetable piece separately. Pick up the vegetable with the long chopsticks, briefly dip into the tempura batter so that it is barely coated, then drop into the hot oil. Repeat with a few more pieces, turning them until golden all over. The tempura are cooked as soon as they rise to the surface; each piece will only take about 1 minute to cook. Remove immediately and drain on kitchen paper.

Serve at once, with curry mayonnaise for dipping.

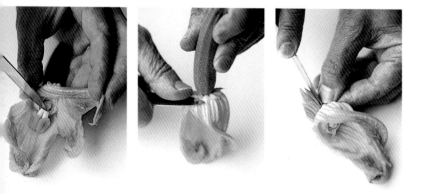

langoustine and squid tempura

Seafood such as langoustines and squid make superb tempura. Cleaned and prepared cuttlefish are also excellent. I serve the seafood in a bowl, garnished with a few deep-fried parsley sprigs, and accompanied by a bowl of sweet and sour sauce (page 24). Seafood tempura is best eaten with chopsticks.

Serves 6

12 raw langoustines
12 baby squid
1 quantity tempura batter (see left)
untoasted sesame oil, for deep-frying
few deep-fried curly parsley sprigs, to garnish
sweet and sour sauce (page 24), to serve

PREPARING SQUID

Hold the squid body with the fingers of one hand and the tentacles with the other.

Pull the body gently to separate it from the head; remove the soft innards. Cut the triangular fins from the body pouch.

Remove the transparent quill from inside the body pouch.

Peel off the purplish-beige membrane covering the pouch.

Using a knife, slit open the body lengthways. Lightly score the whole outside surface of the body in a diamond pattern with the tip of the knife.

Press the top of the head between your thumb and index finger to extract the beak. Cut the tentacles from the head. Squeeze the ink sac to extract the black ink, which can be used in sauces, risotto etc. (Not all varieties have an ink sac.)

Rinse the pouch, fins and tentacles in cold water and pat dry before using.

NOTE Cuttlefish can be prepared in the same way. You will need to push out the cuttlebone from the pouch (akin to removing the quill from squid).

Shell the raw langoustines, removing the head and legs, but leaving on the last ring of the body shell and the tail. Clean and prepare the squid (see left).

Coat the seafood in the batter and deep-fry in the same way as vegetable tempura (see left), allowing 2–3 minutes in the hot oil. Drain on kitchen paper.

Serve the tempura immediately, garnished with deep-fried parsley sprigs, and accompanied by the sweet and sour dipping sauce.

fruit fritters with saffron mango coulis

This dessert is a treat for everyone at the table. The only one who suffers is the cook, who has to keep an eye on the oil and fry the fritters a few at a time. That way, they don't go soggy and the guests enjoy them all the more.

Serves 6

500g firm, ripe fruits (eg strawberries, cherries, small pineapple, apple, banana, apricots, pears)
50g caster sugar
juice of 1 lemon
60ml kirsch (optional)
oil for deep-frying

Batter:

7g baker's yeast
75ml milk
130g plain flour
pinch of salt
1 egg yolk
60ml lager
2 tablespoons groundnut oil
1$\frac{1}{2}$ egg whites (ie 50g)
50g caster sugar

To serve:

caster sugar for sprinkling
saffron mango coulis (page 28)

First make the batter. In a bowl, dissolve the yeast in half the milk. Put the flour and salt in a mixing bowl and slowly pour in the rest of the milk, whisking continuously. Add the egg yolk and lager, still whisking. When everything is well amalgamated, add the yeast mixture and the groundnut oil. Mix thoroughly with the whisk. Cover the bowl with cling film and leave the batter to stand at room temperature for 2 hours.

Peel the fruits and prepare them according to size. Leave strawberries and cherries whole. Slice and core pineapple. Cut the other fruits into quarters or slices, discarding stones and cores.

Put the fruits in a bowl with the sugar, lemon juice, and kirsch if using. Leave to marinate for 30 minutes.

To cook the fritters, heat the oil for deep-frying to 160–190°C. To finish the batter, whisk the egg whites until half-risen, then add the sugar and whisk until firm. Fold delicately into the batter.

Cook the fritters a few at a time. Using a fork and your fingertips, dip the fruits one by one into the batter, making sure they are well coated, then drop them one at a time into the hot oil and fry for 1–3 minutes, depending on their size, until pale golden. As the fritters rise to the surface, turn them over with a fork so that the whole surface is coloured. Remove and drain on kitchen paper. Cook all the fritters in the same way.

To serve, put a crown of green pineapple leaves in the middle of a serving plate and arrange the fritters around it. Sprinkle with sugar, as generously as you like. Serve the mango coulis separately.

casseroles and slow-cooking

These slow-cooked dishes are my favourites in the winter months. They carry the flame of French bourgeois cooking – the product of our countryside. They are the dishes our mothers cooked when we were children – made without much money, but plenty of love. Those were the days …

I have chosen to modify the recipes without compromising or turning my back on excellent old-fashioned, gentle, slow-cooking methods, which are best suited to humble cuts of beef, lamb, veal

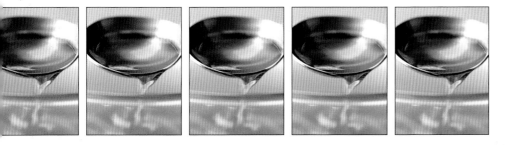

and meat from other cloven-hoofed animals. I have created a blanquette of lamb (page 162), adding mint to make a refreshing, light dish that does not use egg yolks to thicken the sauce; and my modern version of veal carbonnade (page 167) has a light, tasty jus and a colourful garnish of vegetables which marry well with the flavours of the veal. Ragoûts of poultry and game are also deliciously tender and tasty cooked in a casserole with very little liquid.

None of these cooking methods will tolerate an oven temperature higher than 160°C. If you cook on a gas hob, it is essential to use a heat diffuser to keep the temperature at or below 80°C to ensure that the meat becomes tender.

When it comes to fish, particularly salmon, turbot, carp, trout and monkfish, I prefer to braise them in the oven, either whole or cut into large pieces on the bone. I baste them frequently with a little

liquid flavoured with a touch of fresh ginger, saffron, vanilla or curry. When the fish is cooked, I add a squeeze of lemon juice and a knob of butter to the cooking juices, to make a sauce that is glossy and smooth on the palate, then serve this separately in a sauceboat.

In winter, I have a passion for classic cassoulet topped with a layer of chopped pork rinds and fresh breadcrumbs mixed with parsley, which form a delicious thick crust. I have overstuffed myself more than once with this dish, which is *oh so* delicious, but too rich. I can't bear to forgo the pleasure of eating it, so I have resolved to lighten the recipe by replacing the pork and lamb with confit shoulders of rabbit. They are more digestible and add an original twist to this French classic (see recipe on page 164).

In summer, I love tagines, the succulent stews so popular in Morocco. I prefer vegetable tagines, to which I add some fresh herbs from the garden at the end of cooking. Garlic and onions are vital ingredients, adding their special aromas to the vegetables as they cook gently in olive oil – like a fruit compote simmering in its syrup.

Mastering the technique for slow-cooked dishes is easy. All you need is a little time and patience, since they require an hour or two's cooking. Always make sure that the ingredients are not swimming in liquid, but just resting on a bed of red or white wine, beer, light vegetable, chicken or fish stock, or simply water – you can't fail! Most of these dishes will freeze very well and can be successfully reheated in a microwave, so I recommend that you prepare them for six to ten people, then divide them into smaller portions and freeze them in airtight containers to use another time.

vegetable tagine with red mullet fillets

Vegetable tagine is one of the most ubiquitous dishes in Morocco. In Tunisia, they add fish caught by the local fishermen; I like to use red mullet from the Mediterranean. You can substitute different vegetables for those listed; just be sure to start with those that need the longest cooking and finish with the most delicate. If possible, cook the dish in an earthenware tagine, about 30cm in diameter; if you haven't got one, use a heavy casserole instead.

Serves 6

3 fennel bulbs, cut lengthways into 1.5cm thick slices
3 peppers, preferably one each red, yellow and green, halved, cored and deseeded
200ml olive oil
12 white button onions, peeled
6 unpeeled garlic cloves
3 small aubergines, cut into thick batons
3 courgettes, cut into large almond shapes
12 medium cherry tomatoes
2 thyme sprigs
1 savory sprig
24 broad beans, preferably fresh, skinned
6 red mullet fillets, about 160g each
salt and freshly ground pepper
coriander leaves, to garnish

First prepare the vegetables. Blanch the fennel in boiling water, refresh in cold water and drain. Cut the peppers into 3cm squares.

Pour one-third of the olive oil into the tagine or casserole. Place on a medium heat, using a heat diffuser if the tagine has an earthenware base (which must not be placed directly on a naked flame). Add the onions and sweat over a medium heat for 5 minutes.

Add the garlic and peppers and cook for 10 minutes, stirring from time to time, to bring the vegetables into the middle of the tagine.

Add the aubergines and blanched fennel. Add a little salt and pour another third of the oil over the vegetables. Cover the tagine with its conical "hat" or place the lid on the casserole. Leave to simmer gently over medium heat for 15 minutes.

The vegetables will now be half cooked and becoming tender. Stir gently, bringing them into the middle of the tagine, then add the courgettes, tomatoes, thyme, savory, and all but 2 tablespoons of the remaining oil. Cover and cook for another 30–40 minutes on the heat diffuser set over a very low heat, or in the oven at 160°C/gas mark 3, until the vegetables are done to your liking.

Scatter on the broad beans. Season the red mullet fillets with salt and pepper, arrange them on top of the vegetables and sprinkle with a few drops of olive oil. Replace the lid and simmer for another 7–8 minutes, until the fish is cooked.

To serve, just put the tagine in the middle of the table and lift the lid so that your guests can enjoy the aromas of the vegetables and fish as they waft out, and appreciate the mosaic effect of the different colours. Scatter on some coriander leaves and serve.

pheasant en cocotte with crépinettes

This dish, complete with its elaborate garnishes, takes time to prepare, but much of the preparation can be done in advance, so it is ideal for a special occasion. Cooking pheasants en cocotte ensures that they remain succulent, and cooking the thighs separately en crépinette adds a gourmet touch. Of course, you can simplify the dish by cutting the pheasants into portions and omitting the more elaborate garnishes.

Serves 4

2 plump oven-ready pheasants, about 800g each
300ml sweet cider
140g clarified butter (page 188)
1 carrot, peeled and chopped
1 onion, peeled and chopped
1 bouquet garni
6 juniper berries, lightly crushed
salt and freshly ground pepper

Crépinettes:

80g button mushrooms, finely chopped
60g shallots, peeled and finely chopped
30g parsley, chopped
60g crustless white bread, finely diced and soaked in 6 tablespoons milk
1 egg, beaten
100g pig's caul
16 attractive flat-leaf parsley leaves

Garnishes:

2 apples, preferably Reinette or Granny Smith
icing sugar to glaze
8 shallots, peeled
100ml groundnut oil
2 pinches of caster sugar
1 tablespoon wine vinegar
1 small Conference or Louise-Bonne d'Avranches pear
small bunch of watercress

To prepare the pheasants, first cut off the legs. Lift up the skin covering the front of the breasts, remove the wishbones with the tip of a knife and reserve. Using poultry shears, cut the carcasses diagonally, starting below the wings and under the breast fillets. This will cut each pheasant into two parts: the breasts on the bone with the wings attached (like a canoe); and the back of the carcass. Chop the carcass backs; reserve.

Next, prepare the crépinettes. Bone out the pheasant thighs and cut off the flesh. Keep the drumsticks and thigh bones for the sauce. Remove the skin from the thighs and trim off the fat and sinews. Cut the flesh into tiny dice and place in a bowl. Drain and lightly press the bread; add to the bowl with the mushrooms, shallots and parsley; stir well. Mix in the egg. Season this stuffing lightly with salt and pepper.

Spread the caul on a work surface and lay 8 parsley leaves on it, spaced well apart. Put a large spoonful of stuffing on each leaf and top with another parsley leaf.

Cut the caul around each heap of stuffing and wrap to enclose it. Put the crépinettes on a plate, cover with cling film and refrigerate until ready to use.

To prepare the apple garnish, cut each apple vertically into three. Keep the central core section for the sauce. Lay the rounded slices cut side-down on the work surface. Cut into rounds with a 5cm fluted pastry cutter and peel the tops with a swivel peeler. Using a small melon baller, cut out a small ball from the middle of each slice. Replace the apple ball in the hollow, turning it so the inner cut surface now faces outwards to make a "nipple".

Preheat the grill to very hot. Put the 4 fluted apple slices in a small, deep heatproof dish, moisten with 50ml cider and sprinkle with a generous pinch of icing sugar. Cook under the grill for 12–15 minutes, basting them with the juices every 3 or 4 minutes once the sugar has melted. The apples should be lightly caramelised and just cooked in the middle. Take them out of the cider; keep warm.

Now make the sauce. Heat 40g clarified butter in a saucepan, add the chopped carcass backs, thigh bones, drumsticks and wishbones and colour them over a medium heat. Add the carrot, onion and reserved apple core sections. Simmer over a low heat for 5 minutes, then tip the contents of the pan into a

colander to drain off the fat; return to the saucepan. Deglaze with the remaining 250 ml cider and reduce it by half, then add enough cold water just to cover the bones. Bring to the boil, lower the heat and skim the surface. Add the bouquet garni and juniper berries, and simmer gently for 45 minutes. Strain through a fine chinois, return the sauce to the pan and reduce to a slightly syrupy consistency. Season to taste, pour into a bowl and keep covered.

Put the shallots in a small saucepan with the groundnut oil and confit them at 70–80°C for 10 minutes. Drain the shallots, put them into a small frying pan with 1 tablespoon clarified butter and a pinch of sugar, and brown them over a high heat. Deglaze the pan with 1 tablespoon wine vinegar, season with salt and pepper to taste and add the shallots to the apples; keep warm.

Heat 1 tablespoon clarified butter in a small frying pan and sprinkle on a pinch of icing sugar. Quarter the

pear, add to the pan and cook until golden on both sides. Keep warm with the apples and shallots.

To cook the pheasant "canoes", season them with salt, heat 40 g clarified butter in a casserole and brown the pheasant on all sides for 6–8 minutes. Cover the casserole and cook very gently on a heat diffuser for another 15 minutes. Take the canoes out of the casserole, cover with foil and rest for 10 minutes.

Meanwhile, heat 2 tablespoons clarified butter in a frying pan, add the crépinettes and cook over a medium heat for 2–3 minutes on each side.

To serve, reheat the sauce. Take the pheasant breasts off the bone and cut each one into three. Stand the breastbones upright on plates and reconstitute the canoes, placing the meat in its original position. Arrange the glazed apples, pears, shallots and crépinettes around the pheasant, and pop a few watercress leaves in between. Serve the sauce separately in a sauceboat.

blanquette of lamb with mint and a fine egg crust

Simple, light and refreshing, this modern version of a blanquette can be prepared a day in advance and reheated gently on the hob or in a bain-marie. Serve with a rice pilaff (page 93), or plain boiled rice with some blanched sultanas added.

Serves 6

2 boned shoulders of lamb, about 1.4kg total boned weight
300g carrots, peeled and cut into thick rounds
200g onions, peeled and stuck with 6 cloves
1 bouquet garni
1 bunch of mint, about 100g, plus
15g mint leaves, snipped
75g white roux, cooled (see velouté sauce, page 18)
100ml double cream
400g broccoli florets, steamed until crisp
salt and freshly ground pepper

Egg and herb crust:

4 hard-boiled eggs, roughly chopped
20g flat-leaf parsley, finely snipped
15g mint leaves, finely snipped

Trim the lamb, removing all sinews and fat, and cut into 4cm cubes. Place in a shallow saucepan, cover generously with cold water and set over a high heat. The moment the water comes to the boil, reduce the heat and continue to cook very gently for 10 minutes; the temperature must not exceed 70°C.

Add the carrots, onions, bouquet garni and a little salt. Continue to cook at 70°C for 1¹/₂ hours, skimming the surface as necessary. By this time, the meat should be tender and perfectly cooked.

Add the bunch of mint and cook for another 10 minutes, at the same temperature. Lift out the lamb and put into a deep dish; cover with a very damp cloth.

Strain the cooking liquid through a conical sieve into a saucepan, discarding the carrots, onions, mint and bouquet garni. Bring the liquid to the boil and reduce by one-quarter, then whisk in the cold roux, a small piece at a time. Cook over a medium heat for about 10 minutes, whisking continuously to make a very light velouté. Add the cream and bubble the sauce for 3 minutes, still whisking.

Pass the sauce through a fine chinois on to the lamb. Mix carefully, then add the snipped mint leaves. Transfer to a flameproof casserole, add the broccoli and season with salt and pepper. Keep the blanquette warm on a heat diffuser over a very low heat, or in a bain-marie.

To serve, mix the chopped eggs with the snipped parsley and mint. Spoon the blanquette into shallow bowls or individual gratin dishes, sprinkle the egg crust over the surface and serve immediately.

chicken cooked in a sealed cocotte with riesling and girolles

I have adapted this rustic dish to give it a lighter, more modern touch. During the slow cooking, the girolles are almost confit on the pieces of chicken, and the jus is mild and sweet. Fresh fettuccine (page 84), tossed with fine slivers of lemon zest, is the ideal accompaniment.

I always use a fine quality medium dry riesling when cooking this recipe. The house of Beyer in Alsace is renowned for its excellent riesling, which is available from good wine merchants. Of course, as soon as I open the bottle, I have to sip half a glassful to check that it isn't corked.

Serves 4

1 very plump free-range chicken, about 1.8kg, cut into 8 pieces
60g clarified butter (page 188)
16 baby white onions, peeled
300g carrots, peeled and cut into chunky sticks
1 bottle of riesling
80g butter
750g girolles, cleaned
150g plain flour, to seal the lid
salt and freshly ground pepper

Season the chicken pieces with salt and pepper. Put the clarified butter in a lidded cast-iron casserole and set over a medium heat. When the butter is hot, add the chicken pieces and cook, turning them over after a few minutes, until they are evenly coloured all over.

Remove the chicken breast pieces, add the onions to the casserole, and cook with the leg pieces for about 7 minutes longer. Remove the leg pieces, pour off most of the fat from the casserole, add the carrots and Riesling, and cook gently until the liquid has reduced by three-quarters.

Preheat the oven to 180°C/gas mark 4. Heat the butter in a frying pan over a medium heat, add the girolles and cook until they render their liquid. Tip them into a colander, drain well, and season lightly with salt. Return all the chicken pieces to the casserole, add the girolles and put on the lid.

Put the flour in a bowl and add a little cold water, stirring with a spoon to make a softish paste. Use the spoon to spread this paste between the edge of the lid and the outside top edge of the casserole to create a hermetic seal. Cook in the oven for 20 minutes.

To serve, bring the casserole to the table. Break the seal and lift off the lid so that all the aromas of this marvellous chicken dish waft out for the pleasure of your guests.

cassoulet of rabbit confit

In this modern cassoulet, the beans are simply cooked in water, which accentuates their flavour and makes the dish very light. The best dried beans come from Cazères, Pamiers and Tarbes; buy these if you can and soak them in cold water for 6 hours beforehand. If you are using ordinary haricot beans, you will need to soak them for 12 hours. The rabbit confit gives this classic dish an unusual twist.

Serves 4

500g dried white haricot beans, soaked overnight (see above)
1 onion, stuck with a clove
1 large carrot, peeled and cut into 4 chunks
1 bouquet garni
1 small smoked Morteaux sausage (preferably, or a Montbéliard sausage)
2 long chipolata sausages
1 tablespoon groundnut oil
4 confit rabbit shoulders (page 80)
4 thick slices of garlic sausage
6 tablespoons fresh breadcrumbs
2 tablespoons chopped flat-leaf parsley
salt and freshly ground pepper

Drain the haricot beans and put into a saucepan with the onion, carrot and bouquet garni. Cover generously with cold water and bring to the boil over a medium heat. Bubble gently for 10 minutes, then lower the heat, skim the surface and simmer very gently for about 1 1/2 hours.

Blanch the Morteaux sausage in boiling water, refresh in cold water and add it to the haricot beans. Cook for a further 30 minutes or until the beans are tender. When they are, turn off the heat and season lightly with salt, and more generously with pepper.

Blanch the chipolata sausages in boiling water, refresh in cold water and drain well; set aside.

Heat the oil in a frying pan, add the rabbit and fry over a medium heat until golden all over. Transfer them to a plate. Add the chipolatas to the pan and fry in the same way.

When you are ready to serve the cassoulet, preheat the oven to 200°C/gas mark 6. Halve the chipolatas and cut the Morteaux sausage into 8 slices. Remove the onion, carrot and bouquet garni from the beans. Divide the beans between individual deep ovenproof china or earthenware bowls. To each bowl, add a shoulder of rabbit, half a chipolata, two slices of Morteaux sausage and a slice of garlic sausage. Place the bowls in the hot oven for 5 minutes.

Mix together the breadcrumbs and parsley, sprinkle the mixture over the cassoulet, and return the bowls to the oven for 5 minutes. Serve immediately.

cassoulet of pork chops with confit tomatoes

Replace the rabbit with thin pork neck chops. Prepare the cassoulet as above and pan-fry the pork (as for the rabbit) until lightly and evenly coloured.

Add to the cooked haricot beans and simmer for 5 minutes, then add a few confit tomatoes (page 79), and continue as above.

carbonnade of veal with baby carrots and broad beans

This classic dish is traditionally made with beef, but I prefer to use veal, which is more delicate and makes a lighter carbonnade, better suited to my modern style of cooking. The beetroot adds a brilliant touch of purple, which runs into the sauce without altering its character, and its sweet, slightly acidic taste reinforces the flavour of the veal.

Serves 4

1kg boned rack of veal (cut from between the neck and the best end)
80g clarified butter (page 188)
2 medium onions, peeled and diced
2 large carrots, peeled and sliced
250g tomatoes, peeled, deseeded and chopped
500ml dry white wine
400ml boiling veal stock or water
1 medium bouquet garni
24 baby carrots, with their tops, scrubbed and blanched
400g broad beans (weight in the pod), shelled, skinned and blanched
1 beetroot, about 150g, half-cooked until still firm and peeled
salt and freshly ground pepper

Preheat the oven to 140°C/gas mark 1. Cut the veal into 8 equal slices, and season lightly with salt. Put half the clarified butter in a frying pan and set over a high heat. Put in 4 slices of veal, and colour for 2–3 minutes on each side. Transfer them to an ovenproof casserole with a lid. Repeat with the other 4 slices of veal.

In the same frying pan, sweat the onions and sliced carrots over a medium heat for 5 minutes. Add the tomatoes and cook for another 5 minutes. Pour the wine into the pan and cook until it has reduced by two-thirds.

Pour the contents of the pan into the casserole, and add the boiling veal stock or water and the bouquet garni. Cover and cook in the oven for 1 3/4–2 hours. The temperature inside the casserole should not exceed 80°C during this time. Press a slice of veal with your fingertips to check whether it is cooked; it should feel tender and flexible. Gently transfer the veal slices to a shallow flameproof porcelain dish, being careful not to break them. Cover the dish with cling film, and keep warm.

Strain the cooking liquid into a saucepan, set over a low heat and reduce to the consistency of a light jus. Add the whole carrots and simmer for 5 minutes, until they are cooked but still firm. Finally, add the broad beans and cook for another 1 minute. Pour the jus, carrots and broad beans over the veal, place the dish on a heat diffuser, and simmer gently for 2–3 minutes.

Serve the carbonnade straight from the porcelain dish, or in individual deep plates. Coarsely grate the beetroot over the top just before serving.

baking

This type of cooking evokes fond memories of my apprenticeship when, at the age of fourteen, I learnt to handle the baker's shovel in a three-tier oven; it was 3 metres long – twice my own height! The temperature of each tier was different to enable the pâtissier to bake a whole range of cakes and baked goods. Certain pastries require an oven temperature of 160°C, while others need to be cooked at 240°C; the 300°C hottest oven at the bottom, which we called "lethal", was only used for glazing pithiviers, millefeuilles, and the like. The heat it

emitted was so intense that I only had 3 or 4 seconds to thrust in my shovel laden with pastries dusted with icing sugar, and hastily pull it out again before they got burnt – a fascinating experience for a young chef! During the Epiphany period, I had to bake more than 500 *galettes des rois* (Twelfth night cakes) in the space of 3 or 4 days, in addition to the regular daily orders. I was proud of my position as oven-minder; it is a key job, which demands an almost innate skill and a good deal of attention and discipline. Baked goods must be carefully watched; the oven can heat, dry and cook, but unfortunately, it can also burn – and all too often it does. That is why I always recommend using a kitchen timer.

Although this chapter is largely based on classic doughs and pastries – savoury and sweet shortcrust, puff pastry and brioche – I have included a number of original creations, like my crab and rice

noodle quiche (page 174), with its subtle flavours and textures, and my croustade with vegetable spaghetti (page 173), which includes seaweed to enhance the taste of the vegetables. Baked macaroons are delectable served with coffee, and I enjoy developing interesting new flavour variations; my customers at The Waterside Inn adore my novel cinnamon macaroons (page 185).

The step-by-step photographs on page 171 show you exactly how to assemble my tempting anchovy straws, which I can't resist nibbling straight from the oven, at the risk of burning myself in the process ... These *amuse-gueules* are simple to make if you follow the instructions. The anchovies can be replaced with pitted olives, which go equally well with the pastry; better still, delight your guests with a harmonious arrangement of both varieties.

As baking is a process of cooking with dry heat – without liquid or fat – the goods are baked in the tin or directly on a baking sheet. We bake bread rolls, tarts, pizzas, pâtés en croûte etc, and all sorts of small cakes and pastries. Do try my little barquettes (page 178), which are cooled then filled with crème Chantilly and chocolate ganache, to delicious effect.

An oven is a piece of equipment that is in constant use, and it must be cleaned regularly, especially after cooking onions, garlic, fish or anything that spatters grease. Cleaning will prevent the oven from smoking and ensure that your delicate macaroons or brioche are not contaminated by strong, inappropriate flavours. I recommend that you invest in a self-cleaning oven to avoid such pitfalls. One must move with the times for high performance cooking.

rough puff pastry

This puff pastry is very quick and easy to make. You will be amazed at how it rises when it is cooked – almost as much as classic puff pastry. I use it to make anchovy straws (see right), and croustade with vegetable "spaghetti" (page 173).

Makes 1.2 kg

500g plain flour, plus extra for dusting
500g well-chilled butter, cut into small cubes
2 teaspoons fine salt
200ml iced water

Put the flour in a mound on the work surface, make a well in the centre and add the cubes of butter and salt. Using your fingertips, work the butter and flour together, gradually drawing the flour into the middle.

When the butter cubes are half-squashed and the dough is becoming grainy, pour in the iced water in a steady stream, mixing with your other hand.

Continue to mix the dough with your fingertips until all the water is incorporated.

Then gather the dough and knead it several times by pushing it away from you with the heel of your hand. It should be fairly smooth, but you will still see some small particles of butter. Shape the dough into a ball, wrap in cling film and refrigerate for 15 minutes.

Lightly flour the work surface and roll out the pastry into a 30x15cm rectangle. Fold this rectangle into three. This is called the first turn.

Give the block of pastry a quarter-turn, roll it out as before and fold into three. This is the second turn. Lightly press two fingertips into the block to remind yourself that you have made two turns. Wrap the pastry in cling film and refrigerate for 20 minutes.

Give the chilled pastry two more turns, rolling and folding as before. Wrap and refrigerate for at least 30 minutes, or up to 3 days until ready to use.

anchovy straws

These flaky straws are best served warm from the oven – with aperitifs or consommé. Stuffed olives, laid end to end, can replace the anchovies, though the straws won't be as streamlined.

Serves 8

350g rough puff pastry (see left)
good pinch of flour
20 anchovy fillets canned in oil
1 egg yolk mixed with 1 tablespoon milk (eggwash)

Lightly flour the work surface and roll out the pastry into a rectangle, 3mm thick. Halve the rectangle lengthways, wrap one half and keep in the fridge.

If the anchovies are too thick, halve them lengthways. Starting 1.5cm in from the edge of the pastry, lay a line of anchovies along the length of the rectangle. Repeat to make 3 more lines, leaving a 2cm space between each one. Brush the exposed pastry between the anchovies with eggwash.

Take the other piece of pastry from the fridge, lift it on the rolling pin and lay it over the first pastry sheet.

Press firmly with your fingertips to seal, taking care not to press down on the anchovies. Chill in the fridge for 20 minutes.

Preheat the oven to 200°C/gas mark 6. Trim and neaten the pastry edges, then cut the pastry rectangle crosswise into long strips, 2–3mm wide. The pastry strips will be dotted with anchovy pieces. As you cut the anchovy straws, place them on a baking sheet, flat-side down. Bake in the hot oven for 5–6 minutes. If the straws in the corners of the baking sheet are cooked before the rest, just lift them off with a palette knife so that they do not burn. Cool on a wire rack.

croustade with vegetable "spaghetti"

This dish is perfect for vegetarians, and you can vary it by using different vegetables. To make the "spaghetti" the vegetables need to be at least 12cm long, and cooked until crunchy to keep their shape. Try to include seaweed, which enhances the flavour of the other vegetables. Thanks to the astonishing way rough puff pastry rises, the croustade will be at least 5cm high.

Serves 4

750g rough puff pastry (page 170)
good pinch of flour
1 egg yolk mixed with 1 tablespoon milk (eggwash)
100g fresh or preserved spaghetti seaweed
1 cucumber
1 butternut squash
1 daikon (white radish)
1 carrot
2 courgettes
1 tablespoon groundnut oil
4 small cherry tomatoes
300ml sauce suprême (page 18), made with vegetable stock
salt and freshly ground pepper

Preheat the oven to 220°C/gas mark 7. Roll out the pastry on a lightly floured surface into a 17–18cm square, about 7mm thick. Place on a baking sheet and chill in the fridge for at least 30 minutes.

Place the chilled pastry square on the work surface and trim the edges, using a heavy cook's knife, to make a neat square. Cut off a strip, about 1.5cm wide, from each side, taking care to avoid spoiling the shape. Slide a palette knife under the square and carefully lift it on to the baking sheet. Brush the surface with eggwash, then place a pastry strip along one side of the square and brush it with eggwash. Repeat on the other 3 sides, positioning and brushing one pastry strip at a time.

Using a knife blade, make a series of light vertical cuts, about 1cm apart, along the sides of the square, to help the pastry rise as it cooks. With the knife tip, lightly score the raised edges diagonally and score criss-crosses on the corners. Mark leaf shapes in the centre of the pastry, which will become the lid, and prick this in two places with the knife tip.

Bake in the hot oven for 10 minutes, then reduce the setting to 200°C/gas mark 6. Bake for a further 30 minutes, covering the croustade loosely with foil or greaseproof paper if it is browning too quickly.

Using a palette knife, transfer the croustade to a wire rack. Run a knife tip between the lid and the raised edges to a depth of 1cm to cut round the lid. Slide the knife under the lid and delicately lift it.

Meanwhile, prepare the vegetable "spaghetti". Rinse the seaweed thoroughly in cold water for several minutes, especially if it has been preserved in salt. Blanch in boiling water for 1 minute, refresh in cold water, drain and set aside.

Peel the cucumber and, using a mandoline, cut the flesh into long julienne, but don't include the seeds in the middle. Blanch for 15 seconds, refresh and drain. Prepare and blanch the squash in the same way, avoiding the soft central part. Repeat with the daikon, using the whole vegetable. Do the same with the carrot, avoiding the woody centre, but blanch it for 1$1/2$ minutes; refresh and drain.

Wash the courgettes but do not peel. Cut the bright green skin into julienne with the mandoline; don't use the flesh. Blanch for 15 seconds, refresh and drain.

Heat the oil in a small frying pan, put in the tomatoes and colour them for barely 2 minutes. Heat the sauce in a bain-marie and let it bubble for 1 minute just before serving.

Place the croustade on a flat serving plate. Carefully mix all the vegetable "spaghetti" together, put them in a colander and plunge into boiling water for 15 seconds. Drain well and tip into a warmed bowl. Pour over two-thirds of the sauce, mix carefully with a large fork and season to taste. Fill the croustade with the vegetables and place a tomato at each corner. Balance the pastry lid on top and serve the rest of the sauce separately in a sauceboat.

pâte brisée

This light shortcrust with its delicate texture is one of my favourites. It is used for quiches and tarts, such as crab and rice noodle quiche (see right) and salmon mousse and spinach tartlets (page 70). I also use it for fish, meat and pâtés en croûte, like my wild boar and morel pâté en croûte (page 73).

Makes about 475g

250g plain flour
160g butter, cut into small pieces
1 egg
1 teaspoon fine salt
pinch of caster sugar
1 tablespoon cold milk

Put the flour in a mound on the work surface and make a well in the centre. Put in all the other ingredients, except the milk. Using the fingertips of one hand, mix these ingredients, drawing in the flour, a little at a time, with your other hand. When the dough is almost amalgamated, incorporate the milk.

Lightly flour the work surface and knead the dough 2 or 3 times by pushing it away from you with the heel of your hand. It should be smooth and pliable. Wrap it in greaseproof paper or cling film and keep in the fridge until ready to use.

crab and rice noodle quiche

This unusual quiche is creamy without being too rich. It is best served warm, rather than piping hot, to appreciate the delicate flavour of the crab, with a side salad of peppery rocket leaves. You will need a 20cm flan ring, about 4cm deep.

Serves 8–10

1 crab, about 2kg, preferably live, or 300g
fresh white crab meat
300g pâte brisée (see left)
flour for dusting
1 egg yolk mixed with 1 tablespoon milk
(eggwash)
30g rice noodles
1 teaspoon English mustard powder
250ml milk
175ml double cream
3 eggs, plus 2 yolks
salt and cayenne pepper
12 coriander leaves

If using a live crab, scrub lightly to remove any silt from the shell, then plunge into a pan of lightly salted water and cook for 10 minutes. Turn off the heat and leave the crab in the water for 20 minutes, then take it out and leave to cool for at least 1 hour.

When the crab is cold, break off the legs and claws, lift off the top carapace, scrape out and reserve all the white meat, taking care to pick out any bits of shell and cartilage. You should have about 300g white meat. Scrape out the firmish brown meat from the carapace and keep it in a bowl.

Roll out the pastry on a lightly floured surface to a thickness of 3mm and use to line a greased, deep 20cm flan ring placed on a baking sheet. Chill the pastry case in the fridge for 20 minutes.

Meanwhile, preheat the oven to 200°C/gas mark 6. Prick the chilled pastry case in several places with a fork. Line it with greaseproof paper or foil, then fill with dried or ceramic baking beans. Bake in the hot oven for 20 minutes, then remove the baking beans

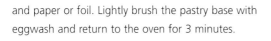

and paper or foil. Lightly brush the pastry base with eggwash and return to the oven for 3 minutes.

Put the rice noodles in a bowl and pour on lightly salted boiling water to cover. Leave for 15 minutes, then drain, refresh and pat dry with a tea-towel. Cut the noodles into 5 cm lengths and mix delicately with the white crab meat.

Put the mustard powder in a bowl and pour on the milk, whisking continuously until blended. Whisk in the cream, eggs and egg yolks, and season with salt and cayenne pepper.

When ready to bake, set the oven to 170°C/gas mark 3. Half-fill the pastry case with the crab meat and noodle mixture, and scatter small pieces of dark crab meat on top. Fill up with white meat and noodles. Arrange the coriander leaves on top, pushing them down lightly so that you can still just see them on the surface. Finally, pour in the filling mixture.

Bake the quiche for 1–1$\frac{1}{4}$ hours, until a fine knife tip inserted into the centre comes out clean. Slide the quiche on to a wire rack and lift off the flan ring. Leave the quiche until warm or tepid before serving.

pâte sucrée

This pastry makes an excellent base for sweet tarts and tartlets. I use it for my caramelised melon and macaroon tart (page 181) and ganache barquettes with crème Chantilly (see right). You can also shape it into small sablés to serve as petits fours. It can be stored for several days in the fridge, or frozen for at least a month.

Makes about 520g
250g plain flour
100g butter, cubed and slightly softened
100g icing sugar, sifted
small pinch of salt
2 eggs, at room temperature

Put the flour in a mound on the work surface and make a well in the centre. Put the butter, icing sugar and salt in the well and mix these ingredients together thoroughly with the fingertips of one hand. Add the eggs, and mix again. Using your other hand, gradually draw the flour into the centre to make a homogeneous dough. Knead it 2 or 3 times with the heel of your hand to amalgamate it completely. Roll the pastry into a ball, wrap it in cling film, and refrigerate until ready to use.

ganache barquettes with crème chantilly

These take time to make, but they are worth the effort. Ideally you need 16 barquette tins, about 11 cm long, 5 cm wide and 1 cm deep, although nine will suffice if you cook them in two batches.

Cocoa butter and cocoa paste give the ganache a superior flavour and texture (see specialist suppliers, page 189); if necessary, you can omit them and use an extra 25g couverture. Any leftover ganache can be shaped into small quenelles and rolled in cocoa powder to make chocolate truffles to serve with coffee.

Makes 8
200g pâte sucrée (see left)
flour for dusting
150g dark couverture, melted
100g caster sugar
16 unskinned almonds, dried in the oven
1 tablespoon groundnut oil
4 marrons glacés

Ganache:
100g dark couverture, chopped
50g cocoa butter, chopped (optional)
25g cocoa paste, chopped (optional)
100ml double cream
25g liquid glucose
1 vanilla pod, split lengthways

Crème Chantilly:
400ml double cream
1 vanilla pod, split lengthways
60ml sugar syrup (page 188)

Roll out the pastry on a lightly floured work surface to a 2mm thickness. Roll it around the rolling pin, then unroll it over 8 barquette moulds. Break off a small piece of excess pastry, and use it to gently press the pastry into the shape of the moulds. Roll the rolling pin across the top of the tins to cut off the excess pastry. Position an empty barquette mould inside each lined mould to act as a press (illustrated above) and refrigerate for 20 minutes.

Meanwhile, preheat oven to 200°C/gas mark 6. To make the ganache, put the couverture, cocoa butter, and cocoa paste if using, into a bowl. Put the cream in a saucepan with the glucose. Scrape the vanilla seeds into the pan, add the pod and heat gently. As soon as the mixture comes to the boil, pour it on to the chocolate mixture, stirring continuously with a wooden spoon until well amalgamated and smooth; do not overwork. Cover with cling film and set aside.

Bake the pastry cases for 5 minutes, then remove the empty moulds, and cook for another 2–3 minutes. Carefully unmould the pastry cases on to a wire rack and leave to cool. When cold, brush the insides with melted couverture (see above), and set aside.

In a small pan, dissolve the sugar on a low heat, stirring, until it turns a pale caramel. Immediately take off the heat and, using a fork, dip the almonds one at a time into the caramel to coat them all over. Place on a lightly oiled baking sheet.

To make the barquette "sails", fit a piping bag with a plain nozzle (ideally a Saint-Honoré). Fill with the ganache and pipe 8 sails on to a sheet of greaseproof paper (see below, left). Refrigerate for at least 1 hour, until hardened.

To make the crème Chantilly, put the cream in a bowl with the seeds from the vanilla pod and whip until it begins to thicken. Add the sugar syrup and beat until the cream leaves a trail when you lift the whisk.

To assemble, fit a piping bag with a star nozzle, fill it with crème Chantilly, and pipe a generous plait into each pastry case. Slide a palette knife under the chocolate sails, and arrange on the cream, pressing down lightly. Place a caramelised almond on either side of each sail, and half a marron glacé at one end.

caramelised melon and macaroon tart

This somewhat extravagant creation isn't a classic tart, but it brings together everything I love – crumbly pâte sucrée, soft macaroons, mouth-watering melon with a crunchy caramel coating, raspberries and kirsch-flavoured cream. You will need a 22cm flan ring, about 2cm deep.

Serves 8

300g pâte sucrée (page 178)
flour for dusting
2 very small melons (grapefruit-sized)
75g soft light brown sugar
500ml crème pâtissière (see right)
200ml double cream, whipped
30ml kirsch (optional)
25 raspberries
8 tiny mint sprigs
7 soft macaroons (page 185), or ready-made macaroons

Preheat the oven to 200°C/gas mark 6. Lightly flour the work surface and roll out the pastry into a circle, about 2mm thick. Roll the pastry on to the rolling pin, then unroll it on to the flan ring so as not to pull it out of shape. Push it into the ring and pinch up the edges to flute them and raise them slightly above the edge of the ring. Slide on to a baking sheet and refrigerate for at least 20 minutes.

Prick the pastry base several times with a fork, then line it with baking parchment and fill with dried or ceramic baking beans. Bake in the hot oven for 25 minutes. Remove the baking beans and parchment, reduce the oven temperature to 180°C/gas mark 4 and bake for a further 5 minutes, so that the pastry is well cooked. Transfer to a wire rack and leave to cool.

Meanwhile, prepare the melons. Cut off the skin, then cut each melon into 4 rounds, about 5cm thick, discarding the ends. Scoop out the seeds from the centre and place the melon rounds on a baking sheet. Sprinkle with the sugar and wave a blow-torch over

the surface to caramelise to a light golden colour.

To assemble the tart, place the pastry case on a serving plate. Whisk the crème pâtissière thoroughly, then fold in the whipped cream and kirsch if using. Pour this cream into the middle of the pastry case. It will subside slightly, but remain in a dome shape.

Put one melon round on the dome and arrange the other 7 melon slices around the cream. Place 4 raspberries in the hole in the central melon round; put 3 raspberries in each of the surrounding melon slices. Pop a sprig of mint into each cluster of raspberries. Finally, arrange the 7 macaroons around the edge.

To enjoy the tart at its best, serve within an hour of assembling, before the caramel starts to melt.

crème pâtissière

I use this pastry cream in many desserts, including my caramelised melon tart (see left). You can keep it in the fridge for 3 or 4 days.

Makes about 750ml

6 egg yolks
125g caster sugar
40g plain flour, sifted
500ml milk
1 vanilla pod, split lengthways
knob of butter, or a little icing sugar

Put the egg yolks in a bowl with a third of the sugar and whisk until the mixture is pale and has a light ribbon consistency. Add the flour and mix in carefully.

Put the milk and remaining sugar in a saucepan. Scrape the vanilla seeds into the pan and add the pod. Bring slowly to the boil, then pour a third on to the egg mixture, whisking continuously. Pour the mixture back into the pan and cook over a medium heat, stirring all the time. Bubble, stirring, for 2 minutes, then tip into a bowl. Discard the vanilla pod.

Dot flakes of butter over the surface or sprinkle lightly with icing sugar to prevent a skin forming as the pastry cream cools.

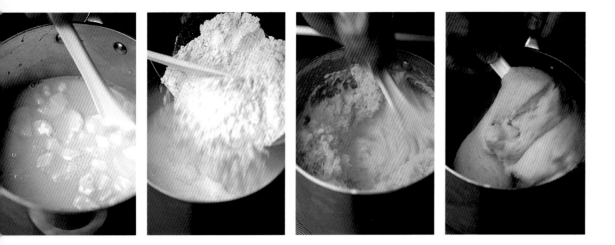

choux pastry

This quantity of choux paste is enough to make 40–50 small buns, or profiteroles (see right). You can easily adapt the recipe to make savoury choux. Omit the sugar and prepare the paste up to the point where the eggs have been incorporated, then add 100g finely grated gruyère. Shape and glaze with eggwash as for profiteroles, then dust with a little gruyère and a touch of paprika before baking. Serve them barely warm, as an appetiser.

Makes about 650g
125ml water
125ml milk
100g butter, diced
$^1/_2$ teaspoon fine sea salt
1 teaspoon caster sugar
150g plain flour, sifted
4 eggs

Put the water, milk, butter, salt and sugar in a medium heavy-based saucepan. Set over a high heat and bring to the boil. Cook for 1 minute, stirring continuously with a spatula.

Take the saucepan off the heat and quickly and evenly tip in the flour all at once, stirring vigorously all the time.

Still off the heat, stir the choux paste until it is smooth and well amalgamated.

Put the pan back on a low heat and stir for 1 minute to "dry out" the mixture slightly. Take care to avoid drying out the choux too much, or it will crack when you bake it. Tip the mixture into a bowl.

Immediately beat in two of the eggs, using the spatula to amalgamate them. Incorporate the other eggs, one at a time.

The paste should be smooth and glossy, and is now ready to use. If you don't want to use it immediately, brush the surface with a little beaten egg to prevent a skin or crust forming, which is liable to happen after a few hours.

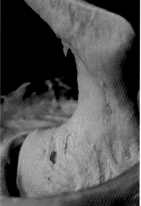

profiteroles with passion fruit crème

These profiteroles are filled with crème pâtissière lightened with whipped cream and flavoured with fragrant passion fruit. For a decadent dessert, dip them in chocolate sauce, or caramel if you prefer. Alternatively, you could simply fill the profiteroles with whipped cream or ice cream, and serve them the usual way – with chocolate sauce poured over.

Serves 8–10
1 quantity choux pastry (see left)
1 egg yolk mixed with 2 teaspoons milk (eggwash)

Filling:
150ml double cream, whipped
1/2 quantity crème pâtissière (page 181), cooled
6–8 passion fruit, halved

To serve:
1 quantity chocolate sauce (page 31), optional
icing sugar to dust (optional)

Preheat the oven to 200°C/gas mark 6. Line two large baking sheets with baking parchment. Spoon the choux paste into a piping bag fitted with a 1.5cm plain nozzle and pipe small mounds in staggered rows on to the prepared baking sheet, spacing them well apart to allow room for the choux pastry to expand. (Staggering the rows helps the buns to cook evenly.)

Lightly brush the mounds with eggwash then flatten them slightly with the back of a fork.

Bake the choux buns in the hot oven for 5 minutes, then open the oven door slightly, leaving it about 1cm ajar to let the steam escape (and allow the buns to crisp). Bake for a further 10–15 minutes, depending on size, until golden brown. Transfer to a wire rack and leave to cool completely.

To make the filling, fold the whipped cream into the crème pâtissière. Scoop out the pulp and seeds from the passion fruit and fold into the mixture. Spoon into a piping bag fitted with a small nozzle.

Assemble the profiteroles shortly before serving. Make a small hole in the side of each choux bun and pipe in the filling. Dip the tops into chocolate sauce to coat if using. Arrange the profiteroles on plates, allowing about five per serving, and dust with icing sugar if you like.

orange tuiles

These wonderful petits fours are so light and delicate that they explode in the mouth. I like to serve them with my coffee sabayon (page 31), but they complement almost all my desserts.

Makes about 20

125g caster sugar
40g plain flour
65g flaked almonds
50g softened butter
grated zest of $^1/2$ orange
50ml strained orange juice

Preheat the oven to 180°C/gas mark 4. Put the sugar, flour, almonds, butter and orange zest in a bowl and beat well, then mix in the orange juice.

Take a soup spoonful of the mixture and push it off on to a non-stick or lightly buttered baking sheet. Repeat to use half of the mixture, spacing the heaps well apart to allow room for spreading. Dip a fork into cold water and use it to flatten the mixture, roughly into rounds. The more you flatten them, the thinner the tuiles will be, but the more fragile they will be to shape when cooked.

Bake in the oven for 4–5 minutes, until the tuiles have spread evenly and are a pale nutty brown colour. Leave the tuiles on the baking sheet for 1 minute, then lift them off with a palette knife and drape them round a rolling pin or a tuile mould so that they set into a curved shape.

When you have moulded a few tuiles, you will need to return the baking sheet to the oven for 30–60 seconds, to soften the unshaped tuiles (which will have hardened on standing). Repeat to bake and shape the remaining mixture.

Keep the cooked tuiles in an airtight container until ready to serve.

cinnamon macaroons

These are excellent served with ice cream or sorbet, or simply with coffee. Like crèmes brûlées, macaroons lend themselves to different flavourings; cinnamon is one of my favourites.

Makes about 30

200g icing sugar
1 teaspoon ground cinnamon
100g ground almonds
100g egg whites (about 4, depending on the size of the eggs)
30g caster sugar
finely grated zest of 2 lemons, dried at room temperature for 2–3 hours

Preheat the oven to 170°C/gas mark 3. Sift the icing sugar and cinnamon together into a bowl and mix in the ground almonds and lemon zest.

Beat the egg whites in another bowl until half-risen, add the caster sugar and continue to beat until very smooth and firm. Scatter in the dry ingredients, delicately folding them in with a slotted spoon or spatula until perfectly amalgamated.

Line one or two baking sheets (depending on their size), with baking parchment. Put the mixture into a piping bag fitted with a 1cm plain nozzle and pipe out about 60 small balls, about 2cm diameter, on to the baking sheets in staggered rows, spacing them well apart to allow room for spreading.

Bake in the oven for 5 minutes. The outside of the macaroons should be firm to the touch, but the inside should still be soft. Leave on the baking parchment for about 10 minutes, then detach the macaroons and sandwich them together in pairs, pressing delicately with your fingertips.

Pile the macaroons into a pyramid in a bowl, or serve them as petits fours. They are best eaten within 24 hours of baking, but if necessary, they will keep for a few days in an airtight container.

brioche

This large brioche is delicious for breakfast, served with jam or fruit compote. It will keep well in the larder for 2 or 3 days – simply warm it in the oven before serving.

Caramelised slices of brioche go beautifully with my poached apricots in assam tea syrup (page 111). Slice the brioche vertically through the "head" with a serrated knife, sprinkle the slices with icing sugar and grill until the sugar has melted into a glaze. This is when the gourmet becomes the gourmand!

You will need a brioche mould (preferably non-stick), that is approximately 20cm across the top, 9cm across the base and 10cm high.

Serves 10–12

350g plain flour, plus extra for dusting
10g fine salt
10g fresh yeast
40ml milk, at room temperature
4 eggs
230g softened butter
20g caster sugar
1 egg yolk mixed with 1 tablespoon milk (eggwash)

Put the flour and salt in the bowl of an electric mixer fitted with the dough hook. Put the yeast and milk in a cup, whisk to dissolve the yeast, then pour the mixture on to the flour. Add the eggs, switch the mixer to low speed and knead until the dough is well amalgamated. Increase the speed a little and knead for 15 minutes, or until the dough becomes smooth and slightly elastic.

Cream the butter and sugar together in a bowl then, with the mixer still running, add to the dough, a little at a time. Continue to knead with the dough hook for a further 15 minutes; by this time the dough will be glossy, smooth and very elastic. Switch off the mixer and remove the dough hook.

Cover the bowl with a tea-towel or baking sheet and leave in a warm place (such as an airing cupboard) at about 24°C for about 2 hours, by which time the dough should have doubled in volume.

Knock back the dough by flipping it over 2 or 3 times with your fingers. Cover it again with the tea-towel or baking sheet and place in the fridge for at least 6 hours, but not more than 24 hours.

To shape the brioche, put the dough on a lightly floured work surface and knock it back firmly a few times. Cut off one-third for the "head" and set aside. Shape the larger piece of dough into a ball and place it in the non-stick or lightly buttered brioche mould. Press two fingertips down into the centre to make a hole in the "body".

Roll the smaller piece of dough into an elongated egg shape. Lightly flour your index and third fingers, place the more pointed end of the dough in the hole in the "body", and press it down into the centre until it touches the base, running your floured fingers all round between the "body" of the brioche and the "head".

Lightly brush the brioche with eggwash and leave it to prove in a warm place for about 1$\frac{1}{2}$ hours. About 30 minutes before baking, preheat the oven to 200°C/gas mark 6. Once the brioche has doubled in volume, lightly brush it again with eggwash. Dip the tips of scissors into cold water and snip evenly around the edges of the "body" in 8 places, dipping the scissors into the water before making each cut. Bake the brioche in the oven for 45–50 minutes.

Leave the brioche in the tin for 5–10 minutes, then unmould it and place on a wire rack.

storecupboard specials

chive oil

Flavoured olive oils are the condiments of the moment. This chive oil will keep well for several days in a sealed bottle, so make plenty and use it to add flavour to grilled fish, crudités or vinaigrettes. Adding a little lemon juice before serving reinforces the taste.

Makes 500ml
500ml olive oil
50g chives, snipped
few drops of lemon juice

In a small saucepan, gently heat the olive oil to about 80°C. Drop in the chives, cover and leave to cool for 1 hour.

Whizz in a blender for 30 seconds, then strain through a chinois into a bottle or jar.

Add a few drops of lemon juice to the flavoured oil just before using.

orange oil

Both this citrus oil and the chive oil (above) are delicious with cold lobster and langoustine salads. To dry orange zests, put them in a cool oven for a few hours; ready dried zests are sold in jars.

Makes 500ml
500ml olive oil
dried zests of 2 oranges
few drops of orange juice

Put the olive oil and dried orange zests in a container, seal tightly and leave to macerate for at least 3 weeks.

Strain the oil just before serving, and add a few drops of orange juice to boost the flavour if necessary.

sugar syrup

This is used for sorbets and other desserts. Crème Chantilly made with sugar syrup in place of icing sugar is more fluid and glossy.

To make 1.4 litres, dissolve 750g caster sugar in 650ml water with 90g liquid glucose, stirring occasionally, then bring to the boil. Boil for 3 minutes, skimming as necessary. Strain the syrup through a chinois, cool and refrigerate for up to 2 weeks.

clarified butter

Melt the butter very gently and ladle the clear liquid through muslin, leaving the milky deposit in the base of the pan.

pickled baby beetroot

These are excellent with cold meats, smoked fish and terrines.

Serves 8
24 small raw baby beetroot
300ml white wine vinegar
50g soft brown sugar
50g caster sugar
1 thyme sprig
1 bay leaf
salt and freshly ground pepper

Peel the beetroot, leaving on 2cm of the leaf stalks. Place in a saucepan, cover generously with cold water, season with salt and pepper and bring to the boil. Lower the heat and simmer gently until tender; they will take at least 45 minutes. When you can insert a fine knife tip into the centre without meeting resistance, the beetroot are cooked.

Drain, refresh in cold water and drain again.

Put the beetroot in a saucepan with all the other ingredients. Bring to the boil and boil for 1 minute. Take off the heat and leave at room temperature for at least 24 hours. Refrigerate for up to 2 weeks.

pickled damsons

Stephen Doherty kindly gave me this recipe. The damsons are delicious with terrines and pâtés, cooked ham and roast venison or pork, and add zing to sauces for game. Like all pickles, they develop character as they mature.

Makes 1.5kg
1kg damsons, de-stalked
450g soft brown sugar
300ml red wine
200ml red wine vinegar
1 cinnamon stick
8 cloves
1 teaspoon coriander seeds
1 teaspoon allspice berries
20g fresh ginger, peeled and thinly sliced

Prick the damsons several times with a trussing needle or fine knife tip; set aside. Put all the other ingredients in a saucepan, bring to the boil and boil for 5 minutes. Add the damsons and bring back to the boil. Immediately take the pan off the heat, cover with cling film and stand it on a rack. Leave to cool, then refrigerate for 12 hours.

Using a slotted spoon, transfer the damsons to sterilised preserving jars. Strain the liquid through a fine chinois into a pan and reduce by almost half to obtain a syrupy juice. Pour this hot juice over the damsons, seal the jars and store in a dark cupboard for at least 1 month before use.

As you serve the pickled damsons, remind your guests to remove the stones.

specialist suppliers

COOKING AND PÂTISSERIE EQUIPMENT

MORA
13 rue de Montmartre
75001 Paris
France
Tel: (00 33) 1.45.08.19.24
Fax: (00 33) 1.45.08.49.05
E-mail: moracontact@mora.fr

CAST-IRON AND CERAMIC COOKWARE AND TAGINES

Staub
68230 Turckheim
France
Tel: (00 33) 3.89.27.77.77
Fax: (00 33) 3.89.27.51.92
Website: www.staub.fr

All-Clad equipment, **Global knives, Tefal** pans and **Braun** appliances are available from specialist cookshops and some large department stores.

CHOCOLATE, COUVERTURE, COCOA BUTTER ETC.

Chocolaterie Valrhona
B.P. 40
26600 Tain l'Hermitage
France
Tel: (00 33) 4.75.07.90.90
Fax: (00 33) 4.75.08.05.17
Website: www.valrhona.com

UK Distributors:

The Personal Catering Company Ltd
D1-D6 Fruit & Vegetable Market
New Covent Garden
London SW8 5LL
Tel: (020) 7498 4000
Fax: (020) 7498 2091

SEAWEED AND SEA VEGETABLES
(also available in many health food and organic shops)

Eco-Zone Ltd
12 Snarsgate Street
London W10 6QP
Tel/Fax: (020) 8962 6399
Website: www.sea-vegetables.co.uk
E-mail: ecozone@sea-vegetables.co.uk

FISH FOR SASHIMI AND SUSHI

Club Chef Direct
Tel. 01275 475252
Website: www.clubchefdirect.co.uk
This company offers next-day delivery throughout the UK

acknowledgements

To my son Alain. We worked together for 20 days to produce the dishes for photography. The result was 200 step-by-step photos and 80 food shots…not one of them needed a re-take. This is pure pride for a father!

Martin Brigdale. After six books together, I feel in such unison with Martin that I want to give the absolute best of myself, as this is what he demands of himself.

Kate Whiteman, who understands me so well that if I have missed something, her translation will cover my omission.

Mary Evans, for her artistic integrity, and her ability to push me that much farther in the most gentle way.

Janet Illsley, who overcame my hesitations of a new member of the side, to prove very quickly that she wanted to give the best of herself and be on a winning team.

Paul Welti, for excellent design work. His enthusiasm was infectious and at the end of a very long day's photography, I cherished the meal the team shared together, as Paul always wore a look of pure joy as he savoured every mouthful.

Helen Trent, for superb photographic styling.

Claude Grant, my secretary and P.A., who gave up a significant chunk of her private time and family life to type and edit my French manuscript.

Robyn, my wife, who spread my vision beyond French cooking. As she applies her natural talent to preparing our daily communal meal, I hardly need venture beyond home to enjoy food from other ethnic origins.

index

steamed poussins scented with ginger and lemon grass, 100–1
girolles
chicken cooked in a sealed cocotte with riesling and girolles, 163
goat's cheese
tender roast vegetables with goat's cheese, 124
goose
roast stuffed Christmas goose, 129
grains, 83
Grand Marnier and mango soufflés, 63–4
grape jus, pigeon canoes with, 146
gravadlax of halibut, 38
green olive and lemon salsa, 24
green olive pasta, 84
griddle pans, 113
grilling, 113
guinea fowl and lamb couscous, 90

h
haddock *see* smoked haddock
halibut, gravadlax of, 38
ham mousse with red pepper salsa, 69
haricot beans
cassoulet of rabbit confit, 164
herb crêpes, 58
herb salsa, 24
hollandaise sauce, 20
horseradish
poached oysters with mayonnaise and horseradish, 102

j
jellied red fruit consommés, 111
jus, 127

k
knives, 11

l
lamb
blanquette of lamb with mint and a fine egg crust, 162
grilled fillet of lamb with Mediterranean vegetables, 116

guinea fowl and lamb couscous, 90
roast leg of lamb with garlic and fresh anchovies, 126–7
langoustines
langoustine and squid tempura, 153
seafood crêpes, 58
leek coulis with saffron and dill, 27
lemon, 9–10
green olive and lemon salsa, 24
lemon and mint vinaigrette, 17
scallops marinated in lemon-scented olive oil, 39
lettuce
steamed fillets of sea bass in green jackets, 99
lime
pear and lime salsa, 23
lobster
grilled lobster with garden herbs, 119
lobster fricassée with peppers, 144
preparation, 144

m
macaroons
caramelised melon and macaroon tart, 181
cinnamon macaroons, 185
mackerel
marinated mackerel diamonds, 38
Michel's sashimi, 37
mangoes
fruit fritters with saffron mango coulis, 155
Grand Marnier and mango soufflés, 63–4
saffron mango coulis, 28
marinades, 13
cooked marinade for meat and game, 14
quick fish marinade, 14
quick meat marinade, 14
sweet-sour marinade, 14
mayonnaise
curry mayonnaise, 20
poached oysters with mayonnaise and horseradish, 102
meat
cooked marinade for, 14
grilling, 113
jus, 127
quick marinade, 14
roasting, 113

see also individual types of meat
medallions of roe deer with green peppercorn butter, 115
melon
caramelised melon and macaroon tart, 181
merguez
eggah with grilled merguez, 56–7
Michel's sashimi, 37
millefeuille of crêpes
soufflées with redcurrants, 60–1
mint
lemon and mint vinaigrette, 17
minted carrot and pumpkin pastilla, 137
monkfish
fish brochettes, 119
pan-fried monkfish with red pepper confit, 142
morels
wild boar and morel pâté en croûte, 73
mousses, 67
celeriac mousse, 77
ham mousse with red pepper salsa, 69
salmon mousse and spinach tartlets, 70
mushrooms
carpaccio of ceps, 43
cep coulis, 25
châteaubriand in a brioche crust, 138
chicken cooked in a sealed cocotte with riesling and girolles, 163
seafood crêpes, 58
wild boar and morel pâté en croûte, 73
wild mushroom cappelletti with herb salsa, 88–9
wild mushroom terrine, 76
mussels
fettuccine with smoked mussels and pesto, 88
lightly smoked mussels, 47
seafood crêpes, 58

n
noodles
crab and rice noodle quiche, 174–5

o
olive oil, 10, 35
chive oil, 188
orange oil, 188

scallops marinated in lemon-scented olive oil, 39
olives
green olive and lemon salsa, 24
green olive pasta, 84
omelette, tomato, 55
onions
poached eggs with fondant white onions, 54
oranges
orange oil, 188
orange tuiles, 185
rhubarb poached in citrus juice topped with coconut flakes, 108
scallops marinated in lemon-scented olive oil, 39
ovens, 169
oysters
opening, 102
poached oysters with mayonnaise and horseradish, 102

p
pak choi, lightly smoked duck breasts with, 44
pan-frying, 141
pans, 11
parmesan and sorrel frittata, 57
passion fruit
profiteroles with passion fruit crème, 183
redcurrant and passion fruit coulis, 28
pasta, 83
eggah with broad beans and tagliatelle, 57
fettuccine with smoked mussels and pesto, 88
green olive pasta, 84
pasta dough, 84
rolling and shaping, 85
serving suggestions, 85
shaping cappelletti, 89
wild mushroom cappelletti with herb salsa, 88–9
pastilla, minted carrot and pumpkin, 137
pastries, 169
anchovy straws, 171
croustade with vegetable "spaghetti", 173
ganache barquettes with crème Chantilly, 178–9
profiteroles with passion fruit crème, 183

pastry
choux, 182
pâte brisée, 174
pâte sucrée, 178
rough puff, 170
pâté en croûte, wild boar and morel, 73
pâte brisée, 174
pâte sucrée, 178
peaches
peeling and stoning, 107
poached white peaches with pistachio crème anglaise, 107
pears
gingered pear coulis, 28
pear and lime salsa, 23
poached pears in Sauternes, 108
peppercorn butter, 115
peppermint soufflé in a chocolate crêpe, 64
peppers
confit sweet peppers, 79
lobster fricassée with peppers, 144
pan-fried monkfish with red pepper confit, 142
poached eggs on watercress salad with red pepper salsa, 54
red pepper salsa, 22
sweet and sour sauce, 24
pesto, 25
fettuccine with smoked mussels and pesto, 88
pheasant en cocotte with "crépinettes", 160–1
pickled baby beetroot, 188
pickled damsons, 188
pigeon canoes with grape jus, 146
pilaff, rice, 93
pine needles, salmon en papillote with, 137
pistachio crème anglaise, 32
poached dishes, 97
poaching eggs, 54
polenta, 83
pork
cassoulet of pork chops with confit tomatoes, 164
roast-poached stuffed loin of pork, 133
potatoes
eggah with grilled merguez, 56–7
little steamed stuffed cabbages, 99
poultry, roasting, 113
poussins
steamed poussins scented with ginger and lemon grass, 100–1

THE LEARNING CENTRE
HAMMERSMITH AND WEST
LONDON COLLEGE
GLIDDON ROAD
LONDON W14 9BL